A GRAIN OF SALT

Joe Cline

authorHOUSE®

AuthorHouse™
1663 Liberty Drive
Bloomington, IN 47403
www.authorhouse.com
Phone: 1-800-839-8640

First published by AuthorHouse 6/25/2009

ISBN: 978-1-4389-8630-2 (e)
ISBN: 978-1-4389-8628-9 (sc)
ISBN: 978-1-4389-8629-6 (hc)

Printed in the United States of America
Bloomington, Indiana

This book is printed on acid-free paper.

PROLOGUE

There is a popular term going around these days, a term that I never heard during my first career as a police officer, "Cold Case". I never really worked a cold case before and never realized the problems associated with them. When you are the new investigator assigned to reopen a cold case you encounter negative feelings from those who were involved in the case during the initial investigation. It is also a problem when several agencies are involved. This case included involvement by the States Attorney's office, the Department of Social Services, the County Sheriff's Department, the medical examiners office from an outside jurisdiction, experts from two outside agencies, two separate hospitals, outside Social Services personnel and my very small town police department. The case was investigated more than six years ago and the decision was made by the States Attorney not to make any arrests due to a lack of evidence. It was now my job to review what everyone did and to find out what he or she did wrong, or what he or she might have missed, if anything, and correct it. You cannot even begin to imagine dealing with people in the criminal justice system from this angle. There are very large egos involved with police officers, attorneys, social workers, and doctors and they usually don't take kindly to someone second-guessing their work. Now take this and add the fact that the new Assistant States Attorney, who was not employed when this case was originally investigated, already has an opinion about who is guilty and expects you to prove it, and by the way their opinion was wrong. There is also another problem with the case. The primary suspect is related to persons with political position in the jurisdiction where the crime occurred.

The investigation of a cold case is really no different than the investigation of a new case. The routine is essentially the same. The collection of evidence and witness testimony remains the task at hand. The problem is that you are dealing with witnesses who must remember what happened a long time ago and the crime scene is long gone. There is also the problem with missing documents that should be in the case file as well as documents that were never obtained in the first place. Probably the most difficult thing to deal with is the fact that you have all of the opinions of those who were originally involved. It is very hard to ignore those opinions as you compile your case file so that you can be objective and let the evidence speak for itself.

I have to say that all of these things presented quite a challenge but nothing compared to the emotional involvement I will experience during my investigation. I have never become emotionally involved in a case prior to this and I thought I was immune to certain feelings while doing my job. As you read this story I am sure that you will also experience some of these feelings. The suffering of a child is probably the most difficult thing for the human spirit to deal with. When you read the details of the injuries that were suffered and relate them to what caused them to happen, it will tear at your heart. When you figure out who is responsible you will want justice. Then you will feel sadness for everyone involved. As you read this story remember that it is true and related factually. It is very hard to believe what people can do to children and this story is but one of very many that deal with abuse, mistreatment and finally murder.

Chapter 1

The Baby Dies

The baby was a sixteen-week-old boy who weighed twelve pounds. He had facial signs consistent with downs syndrome and extremity changes including shortness of fingers. His development was otherwise normal and healthy in appearance. On this day his look was that of a baby about to die. He was flaccid, unresponsive and did not react to any stimuli. His extremities were dark in color and shook as if he was cold. It is hard to believe that his greatest enemy was a few teaspoons of salt. Salt that had invaded every cell of his body and was tearing the life out of him.

The baby took his last breath while his mother, held him in her arms. He never had much of a chance in life and now at just over three months old his life was over. Stricken with severe downs syndrome, liver disease and a hole in his heart put him against all odds of survival from his very first day in the hospital. Nevertheless, he seemed to do very well and after a week was able to go home to live with his mother, father and three year old brother. Every day of his life was a major undertaking for his mother. He was very hard to feed and had trouble keeping food down because of the medications he was on for his liver disease. It was even difficult to get him to feed from a bottle. The deformities caused by downs made it necessary to position his tongue in a certain way just to get him to accept a bottle. Even though the baby's mother had support from her family, especially her mother, it became more and more difficult to care for her family. Her husband was always either working or going out to drink and party with his friends. The recreational life that her husband led used to include her but now with a sick baby and a three-year-old toddler to care for she was never able to go along. Instead, she was left at home with a three-year-old child running around the house and a new baby that required constant attention and care. Even when he was at home her husband was disconnected from his family. He would spend hours working outside on his truck or other projects and would do little to help with the chores around the house.

The home belonged to her husband's friend who invited them in after they became homeless. It was a run down house in a run down neighborhood. The neighbors were mostly very poor and the environment was one of drug dealing, fights in the streets, noisy neighbors and filthy conditions. There was never enough money to go around and the only entertainment provided to her was the occasional affray that could be witnessed through the front window. This was definitely not the life that she had envisioned for herself, especially not at the young age of twenty-four. The baby's mother had lived through three pregnancies, the adoption of her first child, and the continual allegations of the abuse of her children, and the constant abuse of drugs and alcohol by those around her. She had more than one chance to straighten out her life and it seems as if every one of them went in the same direction. All of her problems were shared by her mother and stepfather and caused a lot of stress on their family.

It is often very hard for middle and upper class people to understand the way people live in a very low-income setting. There is very little joy in the daily lives of people who live like this, at least joy, as most people know it. There is never enough food and seldom any new clothes to wear. It is an everyday struggle just to put food on the table. There is the constant complaining to your family who live a lot better than you do. It is hard to get any sympathy from them given that you put yourself in this position when you were a teenager, and continued the same path after they tried to help you on many occasions. You made life decisions that should have been made by someone with maturity. The joy you get is often derived from drug or alcohol abuse and usually leads to even more sorrow in the end. The most common thought about people who are in this position is that it is their fault since they made the decisions that put them there. The truth is that sometimes circumstances cause things to happen and we sometimes take the easy road instead of working hard to improve. A human frailty that I think we are all guilty of now and then. I am not trying to say that any of this excuses wrong, bad or illegal behavior. I just think that it is important for you to understand a little about underlying causes. It is easy for me to understand them. I grew up in the ghettos of Baltimore City, eating welfare food when we had it and little or nothing when we did not. This was my environment until I was twelve years old and my father retired from the military. My parents were divorced and he had little control or interest until then. When he took me away to live in a middle class neighborhood of Virginia I thought I had died and gone to heaven. I was one of the lucky ones I guess, but I still have vivid memories and can sympathize with someone who is living the life I once had.

The baby's mother could be seen breathing a sigh of relief through the tears on her face. The social worker and the nurses that watched as the baby died in her arms felt sympathy for her yet they too felt the underlying relief of freedom from the never ending task of caregiver to such a sick little baby. There was some common curiosity about why the baby's father was not there and why she did not want to notify him that the baby was being taken off life support. It was almost as if she did not want him to know what was happening. She seemed to have an indifferent feeling about the entire situation that day and seemed to just want to get it over with as quick as possible. The previous two days were nightmarish for her to live through. The baby's condition when the ambulance arrived was very poor and the paramedic was very concerned. He was lethargic, unresponsive, and warm to the touch but shaking as if he was cold, his soft spot was sunken in and his hands and feet were dark in color. When the baby arrived at the Hospital the doctors in the emergency room were equally concerned. Then there was the helicopter flight to Children's Hospital and her long drive there while wondering what was happening with her baby. Finally, the words no mother should have to endure. "He is not going to make it and we suggest that he be removed from life support systems." Although, the reaction from the baby's mother was not as expected, she almost immediately responded with what seemed to be indifference and agreed to the doctor's suggestion. When she was driving home that day she had to contemplate what life was going to be like now that the baby was gone, and she had to try to deal with the guilt of what she had done.

The baby's mother never dreamed that during the next year she would see her man leave her and her oldest son adopted, after a lengthy investigation by Social Services into his abuse. She was again alone in life and left with no responsibilities. It was a return to the party lifestyle that she had become so accustomed to prior to the baby's birth. She moved back in with her mother and found a new job and returned to the bars and nightclubs that she knew so well. This was the lifestyle that seemed to suit her best. The only thing different was the everyday thoughts of the baby, his horrible death after such a short painful life, and the ever-present guilt.

The baby's mother continued her daily routine of work and nightly activities of partying for almost three more years. Then she met the father of her next child. This was yet another man with a drinking problem, but he served her needs well until she became pregnant. The birth of her next son presented her with responsibilities that were not unfamiliar. She refused to get tied down again and she had her mother baby-sit while she continued her way of life. These conditions went along pretty well until her man found another woman that he liked better than her. Now she was back in a familiar situation, living alone with a baby to care for and new visits from the Department of Social Services. It seems that more anonymous reports of abuse had surfaced and a social worker was there again to investigate. This led to yet another court hearing and a subsequent order that she could not be alone with the baby until a complete investigation could be completed. The baby's mother was optimistic about the outcome but little did she know that I was looking at her very hard during this time, and that chances were that she would never have custody of this child either.

Chapter II

The Autopsy

To the layman an autopsy is a terrible thing to experience. The foul odor of decaying flesh fills the air. It is an odor that you never forget once you experience it. If you try to imagine, and I doubt you can, the autopsy of a three-month-old infant has even a greater impact on your emotions. I have never been able to completely understand how someone can do this kind of work every day. It is a very difficult thing just to handle the experiences of a police officer let alone those of a medical examiner. I do understand the ability to become hardened, something we all have to do. I have never seen the autopsy of an infant and I can only imagine how difficult that must be to witness. The medical examiner sees many strange and confusing cases in a large metropolitan area especially with the large number of criminal homicides that seem to come in on a daily basis. The baby presented her with a very new and almost unheard of condition for a three-month-old victim.

Hypernatremic Dehydration due to Salt Intoxication is what the autopsy report would read as a primary cause of death. The first question that came to mind was how a three-month-old baby's sodium level could reach 197 when it should be 145. A level of 160 would most likely be fatal to an infant. This led to an intense investigation into the medical records of Children's Hospital by the medical examiner. The first thing noticed was that the baby had been transferred from another hospital and that both hospital labs with identical results performed all of the tests. This is a very unusual circumstance to have a second hospital's records to confirm those of another. It did make it easy to conclude that the tests were accurate and that the likelihood of a mistake was unlikely.

When the baby was presented at the local hospital one of the first test administered revealed his high sodium level and immediate treatment was administered to rectify this. This course of action was continued after his arrival at Children's Hospital. Unfortunately, none of the treatment was effective due to the high level of sodium and its already devastating effect on such a small baby. It was fairly easy for the medical examiner to conclude what the primary cause of death was in this baby. The chance for survival of a three-month-old baby with a sodium level of 197 is almost none. It was also very easy for her to conclude that the cause of death was homicide. Someone had to feed the salt to the baby since a three month old is incapable of feeding itself. The only question that remained would have to be answered by the police, "intentional or accidental".

The medical examiner had not yet made her first incision on the body and it seemed as though the rest of the autopsy would be very routine. In some regards it was routine though, if this would have been a case of shaken baby syndrome. If the medical examiner did not know about the salt and was completing the autopsy as usual, she would have routinely uncovered all the symptoms of shaken baby and it may have been listed at the primary cause of death instead of a secondary cause. The retinal hemorrhages throughout both eyes, the subarachnoid hemorrhage, the falcine and intradural hemorrhages and the cerebral edema that were present in this baby screamed shaken baby syndrome. It was also very evident to the medical examiner that these injuries were very recent and that they occurred within six hours of the baby's presentation to the hospital.

Shaken baby syndrome is a very common occurrence in our society. It is a sad thing to think of someone shaking a baby to the extent that this baby was shaken. In a lot of cases shaken baby results from someone losing their temper and the control of their emotions. It seems that they don't even think of the damage they are doing to a poor defenseless baby. It almost always occurs in infants due to the lack of muscular development in the neck and shoulders and is often blamed on things such as falls or accidental dropping. It is fortunate for law enforcement that the signs of shaken baby are very definitive in nature and unmistakable when they appear. It is also very fortunate that the courts recognize this during criminal trials. If you can show with certainty the person who had custody of the baby when the shaking occurred, you can almost always convict them of child abuse. This case had its own set of complications in that area though. Primarily shaken baby did not cause the death. Even though you can show that it occurred, a jury may be confused by this autopsy report and the primary cause of death.

CHAPTER III

THE REPORT

The social worker had seen many cases like this one. A very young baby that was semi-conscious and unresponsive with no visible sign of injury. Her gut feeling was correct from the very start when she called the Police Department to report the abuse. Unfortunately the social worker did not have a grasp on police procedures and felt that the police department in her jurisdiction would be handling the investigation of this victimized baby. She thought that all she had to do was contact homicide and local Police to report the incident. She did not know that this department would take no action in the case, not even write a report. She also did not know that the local Police where the baby came from would not know that this was a homicide investigation for almost six months later when the autopsy report finally made its way through all of the red tape and bureaucracy and arrived in the hands of the Department of Social Services. This was long after any crime scene could be examined. This was long after the mother and father of the baby had broken up and moved from their residence. This was long after all the interviews of the investigating social worker and the Police. It was also long after they concluded that they probably had a case of shaken baby syndrome but did not have the evidence to convince the prosecutor to allow an arrest to be made. There were too many possible suspects involved and no way to eliminate them. There was also the polygraph of the baby's mother, the most likely suspect, the polygraph that she was supposed to have passed. At least that is what the police were told on the day that she took the test.

The autopsy report was here and it stated that the baby was the victim of a homicide. That the primary cause of his death was salt intoxication and that the secondary cause was shaken baby syndrome. The department of Social Services was able to breathe a sigh of relief since they were out of the picture now. The case was referred to the police for a criminal investigation. A criminal investigation where there was no crime scene, where the primary suspect passed a polygraph test, where the father was totally uncooperative and refused to make any further statements and where there was absolutely no physical evidence to investigate. Then there was also the information that the baby's grandmother was married to a high-ranking County official and that her brother in law was a deputy sheriff. It was no wonder that the States Attorney virtually ended the police investigation with his unwillingness to allow any arrests in the case, even though the probable cause existed to obtain an arrest warrant. The political impact of a States Attorney losing a case like this could be devastating to his career. It is a common circumstance in these situations to require the police to obtain enough evidence to convict before making an arrest instead of just getting enough probable cause to make the arrest and rely on interrogation and follow-up investigation to obtain what you needed to get a conviction. The States Attorney did not want the task of dropping the charges in court if your arrest did not prove fruitful enough to obtain the necessary evidence; it would make them look bad. This would make my job even more difficult. It was now necessary to not only do my job but to make sure that the States Attorney had a slam-dunk of a case to prosecute.

CHAPTER IV

ABUSE?

Six years had passed and at first it seemed like any other anonymous report of child abuse, until they read the name of the alleged abuser. The baby's mother has had another child who was a year and a half old and she was abusing it, according to the reporting person. It was not a difficult decision for Social Services to respond to her home and remove the child until a judge could rule. This was especially true considering the unresolved death of the baby. The judge was not so easily convinced. He ordered that she would not be allowed to be alone with the child until a complete investigation could be done by Social Services. He gave the baby back to her under this condition and set a hearing date for five months later.

The director of Social Services was still struggling with the death of the baby and felt that it was worth trying to get someone to reopen the case. It seems that there has always been one allegation or another that abuse was in the household. The baby's mother has had four children and none of them are in her custody today. Two of the children have been adopted, one is dead and the other is under the care of the court and probably will not be given back to her. The Social Services director called the States Attorney's office and was connected to an assistant attorney who was not working in the office when the baby died. She called a meeting of the local multi-disciplinary team to revisit the case. There was a consensus of opinion that the case was worth looking into.

The Assistant States Attorney organized a meeting of Social Services, the Police Department, the County Bureau of Criminal Investigations and the States Attorney. She wanted to discuss the reopening of the case and the possible assistance of the County Sheriff's office. This was a naïve notion since the Sheriffs Department and the Police did not exactly exist in a cooperative effort. Both a County Sheriff who wanted to control the entire County and a Police Chief that demanded control of his jurisdiction fueled the competition between them.

When the meeting began the States Attorney opened with the statement, "convince me beyond a reasonable doubt". It was very clear to me that he was already resisting prosecution. His subsequent statement that he did not want anyone arrested without a confession made me more apprehensive about this case. I was glad that it was not my case and I was only there as an observer. This was a feeling that would not last long. After about an hour and a half of discussing the case and the very strong opinion of the investigating social worker that the mother was innocent of any wrongdoing, we left under the instruction to reopen the case and attempt to bring it to a conclusion. The original investigator of the case was now my Lieutenant. He approached me and asked me to take over the investigation because it probably needed a new set of eyes. As I agreed to this the thought struck me that I would have to deal with the States Attorney during this investigation. If I only knew then what these dealings would lead to I am not sure that I would have agreed to take the case. The States Attorney wound up being the person in my lifetime that most negatively impacted my family and me.

I then began the task of compiling a complete and chronological case folder that included all reports, interviews, notes, records, depositions and opinions of everyone involved. This was no easy task considering the age of the case and the very archaic and disorganized record keeping system of a small town police department. In 2002 the department went to a new computer system that improved its abilities greatly. Anything prior to that was under the old system and kept in boxes in the basement. If you wanted to see any of the reports it required a hand search that could take hours to complete. There was also the issue of multi-jurisdictional issues and obtaining reports and records from across state lines.

Chapter V

The New Investigator

I retired from a large urban area police department two years before the baby's death. This is a department that is comprised of approximately fifteen hundred officers. I had a career that was varied in assignments. The majority of my time was spent in criminal investigations as an investigator and as an Officer in Charge of an eight man investigative unit. My career was rounded out by a couple of years in Special Operations and my final two years were spent as an Internal Affairs Investigator. I retired after twenty-two years of service and took several years to enjoy life and play a lot of golf. I decided to go back to work when my wife figured that I was bored with life and needed a challenge. It took me almost six months of training to get back my police certification and I had been working cases in my new department for about a year when I learned that I would be investigating a cold case murder investigation. This department was quite a contrast to what I was used to.

It was a department of only fifteen officers in a town that was smaller than most patrol beats that I had worked. It was also overshadowed with political influences at every turn and had to deal with daily multi-jurisdictional issues.

When I was handed the existing file it was a manila folder about an inch thick that contained nothing but a bunch of handwritten notes and a disorganized, confusing report from the Department of Social Services. It appeared as if there were two reports by Social Services and that the pages were mixed up. The report was very hard to understand and the first step I took was to request a copy of the original report sent to me. This is when I learned that the legal adviser for the Department of Social Services was the same attorney who was working for the States Attorney's office and was assigned this case in the beginning. I was also told that he would be consulted before any records were released. I found this to be quite confusing since I usually found Social Services to be very cooperative in past investigations. I learned that the report was a bit convoluted because of a glitch in the computer program that was used to write it. When I received a copy of the complete report it had totally unorganized page numbers and report references. I did find that the text of the report flowed and made sense once read. The most unbelievable thing about the file is that it contained no police report. When I searched the files of my department the only thing that I found was an incident report that documented the fact that the baby was transported to the hospital and the subsequent notification that the baby died. This was a case that was ruled a homicide by the medical examiner and no report of investigation by the police existed. I have still not been able to figure out how this could have occurred. The original investigator told me that he conducted a joint investigation with Social Services and that the Chief allowed their report to stand without a police report. This goes against all procedural guidelines for any police department. There were numerous interviews conducted, some tape recorded, and the police department did not have custody of any of the documents or tapes related to them. This was just the beginning of a quest that lasted for more than two months. The case file did not contain any of the medical records from either hospital. My next step was to obtain the medical records of the baby's treatment at the hospital emergency room and subsequently at Children's. My first thought was to have Social Services obtain these records because they could probably do it without the assistance of a subpoena, and they may still have a copy on file from the original investigation. I called them and made this request and was told that they would have to confer with their legal adviser on this issue. The supervisor at Social Services called me back two days later and advised me that she could not help in this matter because she was told that their case was closed and that they had no authority. I found this interesting because I knew that they were currently conducting an active investigation of this family regarding the current child and that the basis of that investigation was the unresolved death of the baby. It seemed to me that we were working the same investigation, so much for my understanding of the system.

Working a case with multi-jurisdictional issues causes even more complications than usual. A subpoena was needed to retrieve the records from Children's hospital but it was in another jurisdiction and out of state and we did not have normal subpoena power. I also needed to see the records of the social worker that interviewed the baby's mother the day of the baby's death. It was very surprising to me to find out that I still had connections in the Law Enforcement Community and I was able to find out what information existed before I jumped through all of these hoops. I was also able to grease the bureaucratic wheels that would allow records to be released and ultimately Children's accepted our subpoena and they released the records to me.

I discovered through notes in the original file that depositions had been done. A deposition is a transcribed interview under oath. They are usually conducted in an attorney's office with a court stenographer and are very formal in nature. The medical examiner that performed the autopsy of the baby was deposed as well as the doctors who treated him at the emergency room. The deposition of the medical examiner was video taped. The video was easy to obtain because for some reason it was in the hands of the Assistant States Attorney and I was given it upon request. The videotapes of the other depositions were in custody of Social Services and I again went through the phone call where I was told that they would consult with their legal advisor before releasing them to me. This brings to mind another note that I found while looking through the original file. It seems that the Assistant States Attorney who was originally assigned to the case and who was now the legal advisor for Social Services disclosed information from the autopsy report to the baby's grandmother. In effect he told her what had caused the baby's death, salt poisoning. This action occurred right in the middle of the original investigation and goes without explanation. When I read this it raised the hair on the back of my neck and I began to suspect the possibility of political influence causing some of the problems in this case.

After more than two months I felt that I had compiled a complete case file that included all relevant material. I had all of the medical records, the autopsy report, and the ambulance run sheet, depositions from all of the doctors who treated the baby and a deposition of the medical examiner. I also had all of the reports from Social Services, the polygraph report of the baby's mother's test, and my chronological account of everything that had been done up to this point. I had also interviewed the previous investigator and Social Services caseworker. It was now a matter of becoming familiar with all the details of the case. The only problem with this was that the case file had increased from about an inch thick to nearly a foot thick. A lot of the information was repetitive and out of sequence. It was inundated with material that I did not understand including medical jargon and references of a scientific nature. I found that I was also dealing with a cause of death that I have never heard of and that no one that I knew had ever heard of, including the commanders of two major jurisdictions homicide units and all of their investigators. I knew that this was going to be a long road full of new information and educational opportunities. I also began to feel very strongly that someone or something was behind the lack of prosecution in this case. I began to wonder what this would lead to and how I might be affected by it. Little did I know that the effect would be the most troubling thing ever to happen to me during my career as a law enforcement officer and impact my family with undue stress, anxiety and worry for more than seven months.

CHAPTER VI

THE POLYGRAPH TEST

The next step was to attempt to locate the polygraph report. Notes in the file stated that the baby's mother took a polygraph test four months after the baby's death. The notes also stated that when she came out of the test room the polygraph operator told her that she had passed the test. My Lieutenant, the original investigator, witnessed this conversation and in his mind this eliminated the baby's mother as a suspect. The only problem was that there was no copy of the polygraph report in the file. The State Police gave the test and I now had to track down the operator and get a copy of his report. After several attempts to contact him without any success I contacted the quality control director for polygraph reports of the State Police. He informed me that the operator was no longer doing tests and that one of the reasons was his lack of proper reporting techniques. It seems that he was a very good interrogator but a very poor report writer. Several days later the quality control officer contacted me. He told me that he went to the archives in Annapolis and searched the old files for the report in this case. He also told me that there was no case file, which was very unusual. He was able to locate a computer disc in the bottom of one of the file drawers. The computer disc was in an old format that was no longer used and he was attempting to find an old computer that would allow him to download and print the information. When he located the computer and downloaded the information he called me back and told me that he had found it. I asked him if he had a chance to review the test and if he had an opinion as to weather or not the baby's mother was deceptive or truthful. His response was that he hoped I would not ask him that question. When I first contacted him I told him that the information I had was that the mother had passed the test and had been eliminated as a suspect but that I needed a copy of the report for my case file. He told me that he had three other operators review the charts and questions and that in the opinions of all four of them she had been deceptive in two areas. The first was when the baby's mother was asked if she had shaken the baby. She answered no to the question and the charts showed clear deception. The other was that when she was asked about weather or not she fed the baby salt she answered no and it was clear by the charts that she was deceptive. When I inquired how this could be true I was told that since there was no report filed by the operator there was no way to tell what his opinions were. It seems that there must have been a miscommunication between the operator and the police department after the test was administered and since no report was ever filed there was no conflicting information and no one questioned it further. I then requested that the polygraph operator be compelled to write a report and submit it to me. The coordinator agreed that this should be done. The computer disc provided all of the charts and information necessary to write the report and the time that had passed had no bearing on its result. It took me nearly three weeks to obtain this report and I was told by the coordinator that he finally had to go to his commander and request that a direct order be given to the operator to write and submit this report. When I received the report it was clear who had murdered the baby. The bad news in all of this is that a polygraph test is not admissible under any circumstances in criminal court. The good news is that I now had a pretty good idea who shook the baby and who fed him the salt.

Chapter VII

New Territory

I cannot begin to tell you all of the training I have had over more than twenty-five years of work in the law enforcement field. This case caused me to think about it and I estimate that it is probably in the area of four thousand hours of classroom training alone. Although I have had training in the area of child abuse it was never something that I actively investigated. I knew the basics of shaken baby syndrome but did not really have a grasp on what it truly involved. I had never heard of salt poisoning and never really understood how lethal it could be under the right circumstances.

This is where I set two goals for myself as the investigator on this case. The first was to educate myself on the issues of hypernatremia and shaken baby syndrome. The second was to meet the demands of the States Attorney and to convince him beyond a reasonable doubt, as he stated in the first meeting I attended.

I am very thankful for the new computer in my office and the recent installation of high-speed Internet connection. This made my life a lot easier as I sat for countless hours searching the Internet for information. I contacted the National Center for Shaken Baby Syndrome and received valuable information on shaken baby. I never even knew there was such an organization prior to this case coming into my life. Unfortunately most of the medical information I was able to retrieve was full of medical terms that I did not understand. It took me several days of searching to find layman explanations to the conditions involved in shaken baby syndrome. I also spoke with two medical examiners and got their opinions and relevant facts that I needed to understand hypernatremia. An extensive search of the web also provided me with several studies on hypernatremia, its causes, effects and mortality rate. It can probably be most easily understood if you consider a normal adult consuming a cup of salt mixed in a gallon of water over the course of a day then being totally deprived of any hydration. The salt that was ingested would cause severe dehydration as the body finds its need for water to dilute the salt. The only place the body can get the water is from the cells of the body, including the cells of the brain. The removal of water from all of your body cells has a devastating effect that is almost always fatal. I read that it takes only two teaspoons of salt to cause a fatal condition in an average four-month-old infant. I also learned that this was not as uncommon a practice as one would think. There were several recent cases to study and learn about this method of murder.

I have now reached the point where I have all the information that is available from the previous investigation and a fair understanding of the medical condition of the baby when he arrived at the hospital and the only things that could have possibly caused that condition. It was now time to ingest all of the information and look for that one elusive clue that always seems to be in every case, the one thing that convinces everyone of who is guilty, including the members of a jury. It took me just over a week of reading the file over and over again and listening to the deposition of the medical examiner to find my clue. The most compelling thing about the deposition was her description of the injuries related to shaken baby syndrome. Her description of the severity of the injuries and their debilitating effect, as well as the fact that these injuries could only be caused by shaken baby syndrome, kept me up for nearly a week. I was haunted by what the condition the baby must have been when the ambulance arrived to transport him to the hospital. This also reminded me why I never applied to the Child Abuse Section as an Investigator. I knew from the autopsy report that the injuries that the baby suffered due to being shaken had occurred at some time between two and six hours prior to arriving at the hospital. The problem was that he was in the company of his mother, grandmother, father and father's friend during that time. It was my job to prove which one of them had shaken the baby and who fed him the salt that killed him.

This case was very hard for me to deal with. I have always had a soft spot for kids and the hardest part of my job was dealing with kids who were abused. It was always very amazing to me how someone could do the things that they do to children. I have a new grandson who was exactly the age of the baby in this case when I began to investigate it. I had many a sleepless night after coming home from this case and picking up my grandson to hold him. My wife is his babysitter and I saw him nearly every day when I came home from work. I could not help but to think of the description of the baby when the ambulance arrived. He was unconscious, shaking as if he was cold yet hot to the touch because of a fever, his extremities were blue and his soft spot was sunken in. This vision was then intensified by my recent education about hypernatremia and its effects on the body. I knew that this poor little defenseless baby went through a very painful nightmarish experience and as I held my grandson and looked at him the emotion overwhelmed me at times. I have seen a lot of pain during my long career. There have been many gruesome crime scenes visited, autopsies attended, body parts collected at train wrecks and other accidents and things that I cannot begin to describe. I have seen horrific things that human beings do to each other and the terrible results of them. I have never been more disturbed than I have been by the facts of this case, especially as I look into the eyes of my little grandson. The thing that haunts me now is my expectations of adjudication of this case and its outcome.

I wonder what the court will do with this case and what kind of justice will be administered. I think of all the cases that I have seen where there was no justice because of a technicality or because of some political influence. I ponder what would be acceptable to me in this case if I could have my way. I also consider the effects of our liberal society and I know that a lot of people will only be thinking of the anguish of the mother and the pain she must be going through after inflicting such things on her baby. It worries me when I think about the sterility of a courtroom where no baby cries and no victim is heard. I question if I can represent these issues adequately enough to ensure justice will be served. And then I remember; one of the first things a cop learns in the first days of the academy. The job is almost always a thankless one. It is a job that your friends like to make fun of when they talk about donuts, free food, driving fast and getting out of all those tickets for speeding. It is a job where the system attacks your actions at every turn. It is always necessary to maintain perspective and to realize that you have a greater affect on the lives of people than almost any profession. The little things you do will positively influence the lives of a great many people. A cop is but one small part of the criminal justice system of the greatest country on earth. Once your job is done you must take satisfaction that you did it to the best of your ability and that you have little or no control over what the rest of the system does.

This case if different, it causes me to do something that I do not do often enough, pray.

CHAPTER VIII

THE BABY SMILED

The first important thing that I noticed while reviewing the statements of the baby's mother is that she said that the baby became ill around 7:30 that evening. She goes on to say that he was very sick and it frightened her. The puzzling thing was that she waited for nearly three hours before she called for help and then she called her mother instead of an ambulance. It suddenly occurred to me that this alone made her guilty of child abuse for neglecting to obtain medical treatment for the baby. The statute is very clear in this area and I knew that I had enough evidence to arrest her. I became excited knowing that my interrogation skills may enable me to finally get at the truth when I arrested the baby's mother.

I called the Assistant States Attorney and told her of this information and she too was excited by it. She said that she would confer with the States Attorney to get permission to obtain a warrant. When she called me back she was no longer excited and said that the States Attorney would not allow an arrest for this. He wanted evidence adequate to convict someone of murder, not child abuse. I was astounded by this information and became very angry and even more suspicious of the States Attorney and his possible involvement in some kind of cover up in this case. When you consider that this case was more than six years old and everyone knew that the baby was murdered it is hard to believe that the States Attorney would not jump at a chance to arrest a possible suspect. How could he possibly not understand the value of an arrest, even for a lesser charge, and an opportunity to interrogate the suspect under the stress of being arrested? All of my instincts told me that under these circumstances I had a great chance to obtain further information, if not a full confession. This States Attorney was either completely inept or involved in an effort not to prosecute the baby's mother, or both. Little did I know that my frustration and anger which led me to make negative statements about the States Attorney would lead to the worst experience of my life.

I had no choice but to continue to look for more evidence if I wanted to bring this case to a conclusion. I must have read and reviewed the file more than fifty times and I never saw it, until I viewed the video deposition of the Medical Examiner for the fifth time. I listened to the description of the injuries that the baby sustained as a result of being shaken and his physical condition was undeniably very poor after the shaking occurred. I had to narrow down the possibilities of who could have shaken the baby. When I read the file again I saw it, "the baby smiled"!

The night that the baby was taken to the hospital his father left the house to attend a Christmas party. The baby's mother stayed at home to watch the two children. This did not seem to be relevant at first because the medical examiner's estimation of time included two hours prior to this time, giving the father and his friend access to the baby and the opportunity to shake him. The father's statement and the baby's mother's statement both said that when the baby's father and his friend left for the Christmas party, the baby's father kissed him and he smiled. I kept reviewing and saw it again when I read what the father's account was. I kissed him and he smiled at me. It suddenly occurred to me that if the baby had been shaken prior to his father leaving the house it is very unlikely that he would have been conscious, let alone smiling. The baby's mother also stated that she fed the baby a bottle after his father left. I also found it to be very unlikely that the baby would have fed from a bottle given the injuries that he suffered. I immediately called the Medical Examiner and put this question to him. He responded with laughter and said that the baby would not have even been conscious and definitely would not have fed from a bottle after being shaken to the extent that he obviously was.

All of this means that it was now definite that the baby's mother had to be the person who shook the baby since she is the only one who had the opportunity within the timeframe, and it was verified by all statements that the baby was fine when its father left for the party. It also proves that she is the one that caused the injuries that he sustained related to shaken baby syndrome. I now had my probable cause to obtain a warrant for child abuse. I had very strong feelings of apprehension about the idea of dealing with the States Attorney given everything I had already encountered. I went to the Lieutenant who is second in command of the department and requested that he go with me to meet with the States Attorney. This would give me a witness in case something was said or done that may later be important. He agreed and I made an appointment to meet with the States Attorney. I had a strange feeling about this circumstance. In every other case during my career I would be on my way to the Court Commissioner to obtain a warrant for my suspect. In this case I was on my way to obtain permission to do this.

The meeting lasted nearly two hours. I sensed resistance and even anger from the States Attorney while I was explaining to him why I wanted to arrest the baby's mother. It took me nearly an hour to go over all of the evidence and explain my newly acquired knowledge of this case. My gut told me that I needed the element of surprise when I arrested her. I felt that after living with this for more than six years she must have a lot of guilt about what she did to the baby. I wanted to combine the surprise of her arrest with this guilt because I felt that it was my best opportunity to obtain a confession. It was no easy task convincing the States Attorney to allow me to obtain this warrant. It was clear that he was not in favor of arresting the baby's mother. I am glad that I took my Lieutenant with me for the meeting so that I would have a witness. I noticed during our conversation that the States Attorney kept glancing at my Lieutenant and I got the opinion that he was not happy that he was there with us. He would be a valuable witness to anything that was said. After much discussion I noticed a change in the States Attorneys demeanor. He seemed to relax and his entire disposition changed to one that seemed favorable. After the meeting I mentioned this to my lieutenant and he also saw the change occur. His opinion was that I presented the evidence in such a way that the States Attorney realized that he had to get on my side.

The States Attorney said that even though there was adequate evidence to obtain an arrest warrant he wanted me to do another interview of the baby's mother. He said that with this new angle she might confess to the baby's murder. He felt that a confession during a non-custodial interview would be the best evidence for his prosecution. I found this to be very interesting. In order for this interview to occur there would have to be prior notification to the baby's mother and a request for her to submit to the interview. I knew that given her law enforcement family members she would never agree to this and I would only be tipping my hand. There was no question in my mind that she would ask for an attorney and my chances to obtain any kind of a confession would be impossible. I stated this opinion to the States Attorney and he said that this is the way that he wanted it done. I told him that if he wanted it done that way he would have to assign another investigator because I was not going to do it. He looked down at the floor for a few seconds and then said that I was the expert and that I could do it my way. It was obvious to my Lieutenant and me that he was not at all happy about it though.

I was able to convince the States Attorney that the evidence was more than adequate to arrest the baby's mother. In my mind I wanted to ask why no one had come to this conclusion six years earlier since the evidence was always there. During my investigation I did not interview any suspects, visit any crime scene, uncover any new evidence or work any special magic. All I did was read the existing file and point out facts that any competent investigator should have seen.

When I left his office I went directly to the District Court Commissioner with the warrant applications that I had already completed prior to meeting with the States Attorney. I obtained the warrants and set up surveillance. I had some concern that the baby's mother may hear of this before I could arrest her. I needed to get her alone so that I could make the arrest while she was not under the influence of her family who I believe would have advised her not to talk to me. The most powerful tool of a criminal investigator is a custodial interrogation of the suspect, an interrogation where the suspect feels all alone and surprised. I felt that given these circumstances I had a very good chance to obtain a truthful statement.

Chapter IX

The Arrest

I watched the house for seven hours that night, until it was evident that everyone had gone to bed. I returned the next morning at five o'clock and found that the baby's mother's car was still in the driveway. After three hours of waiting she came out of the house and got into her car with her older daughter. I figured that she was taking her to school and I was correct. I followed her so that I could wait until she dropped her off. I did not want to traumatize this child unnecessarily. After she dropped her off I called for a uniform unit to make the stop. When I walked up to her car I saw her for the very first time. She impressed me as an average looking woman who was a bit overweight and dressed in casual loose fitting clothing. She looked like any woman you might see walking down the street or in a shopping mall. I could not help but to think to myself how hard it was to believe that she could have done what she did to her baby. I told her my name and advised her that I had a warrant for her arrest. I needed to be very careful not to engage in any conversation with her that was accusatory in nature. I hoped that she might make some statements on her own. Under these circumstances her statements would be admissible during a trial. The baby's mother had a confused look on her face but said nothing at all and I placed her into handcuffs and into the front seat of my car. When I began to drive to the station she asked me what it was about. I told her it was about the death of the baby. She became very upset and said, "I passed the polygraph". She kept repeating this until I told her that there was a mistake and that she did not pass the polygraph. The impact of this information was emotionally devastating to her. She broke down and began to cry very hard. It was very obvious to me that she had a lot of guilt stored up inside after six years of daily reminders of December 19, 1998, a day she will never be able to forget. While we were driving I was trying to get a read on her and decide weather or not her tears were those of fright or tears of someone who realized that they had finally been caught. All of my experience told me that it was the latter. I say this because she was not objecting or verbally defending herself. Instead, she appeared to be thinking hard and trying figure out what to do next. She said that he was her miracle baby and she could not believe that anyone would think that she would hurt him. The Miranda rights were very easy to get through. The baby's mother said that she had nothing to hide and would be glad to talk to me. This was a strange thing for a woman to say considering the fact that she could hardly say it through the tears and blubbering. My experience told me right away that she was guilty and that she would probably admit to it.

Chapter X

The Interrogation

The successful interrogation of a criminal suspect is a true art form. It is an ever-evolving process of learning. A very seasoned detective once told me that a lot of cops don't realize that you can beat down a suspect with a stick today, and tomorrow he will present you with the same problems. When you break someone in an interrogation room they are yours for life. There are many different methods of interrogation that can be used on a suspect. The problem is having the experience to know which to use and which not to use. I felt in the baby's mother's case that the guilt about what she did to the baby was my best tool to use against her. I figured that if I simply laid out the evidence in a way that she could understand it she would come to terms with the reality of the charges against her. A lot of times when someone feels a lot of guilt they have a very strong desire to confess and relieve themselves of the burden that they carry. I read the baby's mother as a very weak minded person and someone who was very likely to be in this category.

An interrogation room is ideally a very small room with very little in it; preferably about six by eight feet in size containing only two chairs. This way the interrogator can be close to the suspect and get into their space. This is the best place to be when you are applying pressure and it can also be beneficial if you are trying to build trust and create a rapport with them. It is also essential that they have no distractions. Anything that they might focus on could help them to avoid what you are trying to do.

The interrogation room we used was exactly like this. It used to be a bathroom and was converted just a few months prior to the baby's mother's arrest. I took her into the room and had her sit in one of the chairs and left her, closing the door behind me. I left her alone for thirty minutes so that she could think about her situation and hopefully get the mindset that she would do almost anything to get out of her dilemma. I had a lot of things in my favor. She had dodged being arrested for six years and probably felt that she could continue to avoid prosecution. She was alone with no one to lean on or to get advice from. She was very frightened and could be easily intimidated. I also avoided telling her what the exact charges on the warrant were. If I told her that they were for child abuse and not murder I felt that this would cause her not to talk about the administration of salt to the baby.

I started with the polygraph report and the charts and questions from the test. I showed them to her and explained how they were read. I told her about the autopsy report and the conclusions of the medical examiner as to the time that the baby was shaken. I explained how everyone else could be eliminated because of the time frame. As I finished explaining she began to cry again and said that she might have shaken him but it was so long ago she did not remember. I told her that I did not believe her and that I knew that that day was the worst day of her life and that she would never forget one moment of it. She really began to cry at this point and said, "OK, I shook him, I did not mean to hurt him." This was a hard thing for her to admit but it was obvious that admitting it gave her instant relief of more than six years of grief. As I continued, I began to talk about denying the baby medical help after it was obvious that he was injured. She became more indifferent and said that she was scared because he looked so sick and she did not know what to do. I asked her why she waited for over two hours and then called her mother instead of an ambulance. I described how the baby looked and how obviously sick he was. She said that she was afraid and her mother always helped her when her kids were sick. She kept saying that she was scared to call anyone else because the baby looked so bad.

I now had confessions for three separate charges, two counts of child abuse and one count of first-degree assault. One count of child abuse was for the admission that she had shaken the baby, and one was for failing to provide medical attention. These charges carried total maximum penalties of forty years in jail. My next goal was to obtain a confession for administering salt to the baby, which was the primary cause of his death. I began to talk about this issue and the baby's mother became very defensive and angry. She denied putting salt into the baby's formula. The only problem is that I did not mention anything about putting salt into his formula; I only asked her if she had anything to do with him being given the salt. She went on talking and said that she had found her three year old playing with the formula and he had it spilled on the floor. She said that maybe he put the salt in the formula without her knowing it. I reminded her that she had previously made statements that she was the only one who fed the baby that day and she said that she was the only one who ever fed him. She previously explained that his downs prevented him from receiving a bottle and that she had to pull his tongue out and put the nipple in his mouth. She also said that she was the only one who could do this and no one else ever fed him. I then asked her if her mother helped her to give the baby the salt. This caused her to begin to cry again and she asked for a lawyer. She said that she could not do this without a lawyer. A person's rights guarantee them the right to an attorney when they are being questioned. Even though the baby's mother waived this right in the beginning of the interview when she asked for a lawyer she automatically invokes this right again. This ended the interview and my ability to ask her any further questions.

I found her response about her son putting salt in the formula quite suspicious and I will always be of the opinion that this is the way the salt was given to him. The only problem is that it is one thing to believe something and another thing to prove it. The remote possibility exist that someone other than the baby's mother put salt into his formula and did it without her knowledge, even though there is no known motive for this. I also felt suspicious about how she shut down when I mentioned her mother. I have always felt that someone may have either helped the baby's mother give him salt or possibly suggested it to her as a means of getting rid of the baby. I was told that her mother used to be some kind of medical aid and I wondered if she might have this knowledge about the affect of giving a baby salt. I have no evidence of anyone assisting the baby's mother but I will always wonder.

The bond that was set seemed to be quite low considering the three felony charges. The bond was set at $25,000. When the bond review was brought before a judge he told the assistant states attorney that he had a problem with the age of the case and was considering releasing her on her own recognizance. When the circumstances of the case were given to the judge he decided to uphold the bond but her family bonded her out the same day.

CHAPTER XI

JAILHOUSE RAT

It has been my experience that when someone is guilty of a very serious crime they have an uncontrollable urge to talk about it and to try to rationalize what they did. This is especially true among people who are locked up in jail together. I don't know why it is but for some reason they feel secure about talking about things they have done. I guess it goes back to the old saying about honor among thieves. The truth of the matter is that someone who is in jail will use just about anything they can to better their situation. I got a call one day and was told that apparently while the baby's mother was in jail after I arrested her she talked to her cellmate about this case. I was also told that the States Attorney had received a letter from this cellmate that said she had some information about the case. When I received this information it was five days old. For reasons unknown to me the States Attorney did not notify me about this information but I found out that his investigator was going to interview this cellmate. I found this to be a little curious considering it was my investigation and I had done all of the work up to this point. I called the States Attorney to discuss other information about the case hoping that he would disclose this to me. After talking about another issue he did in fact tell me about the letter and that his investigator had interviewed the cellmate about it. The following day I was in court and had reason to go into the States Attorneys office. I was called into the investigators office and given a copy of his report regarding the interview and was allowed to read the letter that they received. He also told me that the States Attorney was leaning toward presenting the case to the grand jury in an attempt to get an indictment for murder. It seems that the baby's mother had made statements about giving the baby salt to relieve him of constipation and that may be why his sodium level was high. This testimony would be very harmful since it gives some corroboration to other circumstantial evidence in the case. There may now be a good chance for a jury to convict of a murder charge.

It still bothers me that I was not immediately informed by the States Attorney about this information. I am the most knowledgeable person when it comes to this case and should be the likely one to interview the cellmate. I am starting to see things like this surface though. I have also not read my name in any of the local newspaper articles. It seems that all of the press releases contain the name of the States Attorney and that gets published. This is a case that could have a great potential for political gain for the States Attorney and it looks like we are headed in that direction. It really does not concern me if I get credit for this case or not, but it does concern me that political motivations may steer the prosecution instead of a motivation to obtain justice. I have seen this before and it sometimes has the wrong result in the end.

Chapter XII

The Preliminary Hearing

When the baby's mother was arrested and placed on $25,000 bond she was scheduled for a bond review in front of a District Court judge. The States Attorney, in a very rare move, drove to the courthouse to conduct the bond review hearing personally. An assistant normally conducts these hearings. The judge was concerned with the age of the case and wanted to know why it took more than six years for her to be charged. The States Attorney explained that the evidence was not present until recently and the police did not have cause to charge her. The fact is that the evidence was present all the time. It was there from the day after the baby died and the mother was interviewed. Anyway, now she has been charged and the States Attorney seems to be handling the case himself. This is really easy to understand given the likelihood that the case will receive a lot of media coverage and we are in an election year.

It has only been 11 days since the baby's mother's arrest and I have already received a summons for the preliminary inquiry. I find this a little curious since it usually takes about three weeks for this to happen. As a matter of fact I have two armed robbery cases that I made an arrest on the week prior to arresting the baby's mother and I have not received notice on either of them yet. This is yet another curious happening that makes it appear as if someone is pushing buttons in the system. Maybe this is just my imagination.

The court system is divided into two courts, the district court and the circuit court. The district court hears most of the minor crime violations and the circuit court hears the more serious ones. Whenever someone is charged with a serious crime that is not in the jurisdiction of the district court a hearing must be conducted to establish that probable cause exist to prosecute the case in the higher court. This is called a preliminary hearing. During the preliminary hearing the arresting officer testifies to all of the evidence collected against the defendant. The officer may even testify to hearsay evidence and describe physical evidence without having to present it to the court. The district court judge then determines weather or not the case has merit and sends it to the circuit court for prosecution. This hearing also provides an opportunity for the defense attorney to hear what evidence exist against his client. It also provides him with an opportunity to see the arresting officer testify and to find out the quality of his skills in this area. This can prove to be very fruitful when it comes time to go to trial. Testifying in court is a very stressful experience, especially in a case such as this one. There is a lot of evidence in this case and a great amount of necessary testimony to present it. I have testified so many times that I cannot remember half of them, but I must admit I am nervous about this case. With all of the overshadowing issues and the pressure of media attention the stress level increases significantly.

On the day of the scheduled preliminary hearing I was approached by the public defender that stated that he was representing the baby's mother. He said that he was going to request a continuance for a period of thirty days. The purpose of this continuance was to obtain copies of the medical records that I referred to in the statement of probable cause that was used to obtain warrants for her arrest. This request was an obvious ploy to delay this case. Since I would be the only one who testifies in a preliminary hearing and I can't testify to any medical issues, it would have little or no benefit to the public defender to obtain these records. The fact is though that it sounds like a reasonable request and it would give the public defender a month to review the case. Considering the voluminous content of the file this is probably advisable from the defense attorney's point of view.

When I went into the courtroom I did not see the baby's mother there. Just prior to the judge entering the room she walked in the front door and was alone. She took a seat by herself and I wondered where her family was. It was about ten minutes later that her uncle, the deputy sheriff entered the courtroom and took a seat beside her. About ten minutes after that her mother appeared and joined them. It was about fifteen minutes later that her stepfather arrived; he is the high-ranking official in the county jail. I thought it to be interesting that they were all here for this minor event, especially since the public defenders plan was to get a continuance. It seems as if I will have to deal with the presence of these family members throughout the remainder of the case. This is difficult since her family is deeply entrenched in the law enforcement community and I know them through my job. I feel a sense of sadness when I watch them go through what must be a very painful and traumatic experience. I also think of the very good possibility of impending murder charges. This is something that they are probably not aware of yet. Of course I say that with the thought in mind that they seem to have been aware of every step that was taken in the initial investigation and I am not so naive to believe that they don't know everything that I do. These feelings will be ever present through this trial, at least until its conclusion.

The judge granted the request of the public defender for a thirty-day continuance. It was obvious that the public defender did not have a clue of the possibility of the States Attorney presenting this case to the grand jury for indictment. If the grand jury does in fact indict her, the preliminary hearing would be a moot point and all charges as they stand would be dropped in favor of the indictments. I am really hoping that this occurs and the grand jury sees fit to indict for murder and other related charges.

Chapter XIII

The States Attorney

The States Attorney in my jurisdiction is quite a story in itself. He is currently in his second term of office. He was originally an assistant when the sitting States Attorney retired during his elected term. The current States Attorney was appointed to fill the job until the next election. During the next two election cycles he had one opponent disqualified for a lack of proper residency requirement and offered another opponent the chief deputy job if he would withdraw from the race. It seems that he must have had a lack of confidence in his ability to get the support he needed. I remember the first time I met him. My Chief had me attend a breakfast given by the State Municipal organization. There were many important people in attendance including all the local politicians and the Lieutenant Governor of the State. I was very new in this crowd and sat at a table for eight people that only had one person sitting there. This person introduced himself to me as the States Attorney. It never occurred to me that he was THE States Attorney. I assumed that he was an assistant. I never gave it much thought until I got involved in this case and I remembered this day. It occurred to me that it was very strange that he was sitting by himself and not given a seat at one of the VIP tables. I also noticed that he did not get very much attention from others that were in attendance either. Maybe you can figure this out as you continue to read this story. You should keep in mind that the person who holds this position is all-powerful. He is exempt from civil prosecution resulting in any prosecutorial decision he makes. He is also exempt from criminal prosecution unless there is very compelling evidence to support any allegations. It makes you virtually powerless if he does things to you that are unfair or even out of moral bounds. This is a very necessary condition when it is confined to prosecutions that are ethically, morally and fairly administered. It is also a very bad thing if the person in power uses his power in ways that are not what the lawmakers intended when they gave the position so much power.

Chapter XIV

The Grand Jury

When I discussed the information with the States Attorney about the cellmate he told me that he would be in touch with me and let me know how he was going to proceed. After two weeks passed I did not hear from him until I received a subpoena to testify before the grand jury. I received this document with several mixed emotions. My first reaction was disappointment that the States Attorney did not contact me and inform me of his decision to present the case for indictment. After a few seconds of reflection I brought myself back to reality. It is becoming ever more apparent that the States Attorney intends to use this case for his political benefit. This plan is all right with me and I understand his motives and needs to go in this direction. It is nonetheless disappointing that he does not include me in the process in a more friendly way. It is almost as if he does not trust me enough to give me information about things before they happen. After coming to grips with this issue I began to feel a great sense of satisfaction and pride. I know that this subpoena means that the States Attorney intends to seek charges of murder against the baby's mother. I also know that it is very likely that the Grand Jury will return indictments charging with murder and other related crimes. This action is a long time coming and regardless of the outcome of the trial I will have the sense of relief that every cop gets when he knows that his part of the judicial equation has been fulfilled by his hard work and persistence. When a States Attorney takes a case to the Grand Jury he also assumes the responsibility for the prosecution of the case and this gives me relief to know that my job is complete except for the testimony I will give at the trial.

I am sitting here on the day that I received the subpoena for the Grand Jury and writing this chapter. I go through every day of my life these days thinking of this case and how it will proceed. The case has made the local newspapers and it seems that every time I go somewhere I get questions and congratulations from someone. I just got off of the phone with the local television station regarding another case. I have established a relationship with one of the reporters and she has questioned me about this case. The only thing that I have been able to tell her is to make sure she follows the case because it will become very newsworthy in the near future. This of course causes her to go crazy with curiosity and she fires questions at me that I can't answer. I just tell her that the end is near and she will get her story.

I am now five days prior to my testimony in front of the Grand Jury. The Grand Jury is comprised of twenty-two

A Grain of Salt

citizens. It is necessary to convince twelve of them that a suspect should be charged with a crime. In all probability I will be the only witness who testifies in this case. This means that I will have to tell the complete story, even the part prior to my involvement, including all medical information. I will have to explain all evidence in the case so that a layperson can understand it and relate it to their decision. As I sit here looking at the case file that has evolved from a foot thick pile to a full five inches thick organized and detailed account of the case. I wonder how I will do under the pressure of testifying. I normally do not get too overly stressed out about testifying but this case is unusually important to me and I want to get it right. The most curious thing is that I have not yet heard from the States Attorney about the Grand Jury testimony. I would think that he would find it necessary to meet with me to discuss what information is important to provide and what information to try to stay away from. This is especially true in such a complicated and unusual case. I just got off the phone with the Assistant States Attorney who has been handling this case and she knows nothing more than I do. She is apparently involved in another case and will not be able to handle the Grand Jury presentation. I may not know the answers to any of these questions until I get on the stand. Nothing about this case has been easy, why should this be different.

On the day prior to my Grand Jury appearance I had still not heard from the States Attorney about a conference with him to prepare for this testimony. I had my Chief call him and ask about it and he said for me to come to his office in a couple of hours if I needed to discuss it. We had a rather long conversation and discussed many of the issues of the case.

Apparently he did not have any concerns and was prepared to go forward without meeting. I felt it necessary to make sure that I did not enter any areas that he did not want me to.

On the day of Grand Jury testimony I was the first witness called to testify. I spent nearly two hours telling the story to them and then answered many questions. There were twenty-two jurors and we needed to convince twelve of them to obtain an indictment. After my testimony the cellmate testified as to what the baby's mother told her about giving the baby salt and or sugar. The social worker then testified for about a half an hour and the Grand Jury was then sent to deliberate. After less than an hour they returned with indictments for first-degree murder, child abuse and first-degree assault. I later found out that their vote to indict was 21 for and only one against.

Chapter XV

Arrested Again

I met with the States Attorney after the indictment was returned by the Grand Jury and presented to the Circuit Court Judge. The Judge ordered a warrant for the baby's mother and now she had to be arrested again, this time it would be for first-degree murder and she would be facing a life sentence.

Every county has a Sheriff's department, which has a primary duty of carrying out all orders of the court, including serving its arrest warrants when issued from the bench. I requested that the States Attorney allow me to serve the warrant and arrest the baby's mother because I felt that she might make voluntary statements that could be valuable as prosecutorial evidence. Even though she had an attorney and I was not allowed to interview her without him being present, she could still make any statement that she wanted to so long as it was not a response to my questions. The States Attorney agreed that this was a viable issue but said that it was the Sheriff's department's job to serve the warrant. He does however have the power to allow me to serve the warrant on my own. This is only a procedural issue not a legal issue. Even though I tried to explain to him the importance of my control over this arrest he would not waiver. I knew in my own mind that there was a great probability that when the Sheriff's Department got this warrant to serve, the baby's mother would know that they were coming prior to their arrival. This would give her an opportunity to be coached on how to act and what not to say. He agreed to call the Sheriff's Department and tell them that he would like me to be present during the arrest in case she gave any relevant information. He made the call to the Captain in charge while I was in his office and he was told that this would be all right. I gave him my cell phone number and the States Attorney requested that I be called when they were going to make the arrest so that I could be present.

It was about three hours later when my cell phone rang and a female deputy said that she was in route to serve the warrant and asked where I would like to meet her. I requested that she come by my station and she agreed. When she arrived she stated that she was going to the home of the baby's mother and I told her that she would not be there and that she would be at her mother's house here in town. I then told her that I wanted to ride with her so that I could be present during the entire arrest process. She said that her Captain instructed her to allow me to be present during the arrest but not be allowed to come to their office where she would be processed. I told her that it was very important that I was present through the entire process and she said that she would call her Captain.

She made the call from her cell phone in her car and he told her that I could not come to their office because the baby's mother's uncle was working there and he did not want any confrontation to occur. It was now after hours and I knew that it would take me quite some time to get a hold of the States Attorney so I decided not to resist this denial.

When we arrived at the residence and the deputy knocked on the door it was answered by the baby's grandfather who greeted the deputy by her first name. When she told him why we were there he allowed us to come in and then he began to become very angry. He shouted at the baby's mother and told her not to say anything and then he pointed at me with anger and said, "Don't say anything to that man". This was a very difficult situation for me. Anytime you are put in the position of arresting a close relative of a law enforcement officer the thrill of victory is overshadowed by the compassion that you feel for them. I have experienced these feelings during this entire investigation and it has made it very hard for me to do the things that usually come very naturally. When you conclude a murder investigation with an arrest of the suspect and the knowledge that you have gathered the evidence necessary to convict it usually brings you a great feeling of satisfaction. In this case the feelings were bitter sweet to say the least. I only hope that the family reads this and understands that I have great sympathy for what they are going through and tremendous feelings of sadness, concern and caring for them.

The baby's mother was processed and taken before the District Court Commissioner for a hearing. She was jailed with no bond and is not entitled to a bond hearing with a charge of murder. She will most likely sit in a jail cell until the day of the trial, two to three months away. I have to think that she is having thoughts that she is finally going to pay for what she has done. It has now been more than six years since it happened and living with the guilt every day has to have been very hard. Now all that is left for her is to sit and wait for the trial and the conclusion to this segment of her life.

CHAPTER XVI

THE MEDIA

When the press release was done the phone began to ring. This is only the second murder trial case in the County in the past eight years. It is a very unusual and newsworthy circumstance. Several local reporters interviewed me and it was very difficult not to give them any information about the case more than the arrest date and the charges. As we all know the media can have a great affect on the outcome of a criminal trial. I cannot tell you how many times during my career that I have been interviewed about a case and then when I see the article in the paper the next day wonder what they are talking about. The media has one priority, sell their product. It has been my experience that some reporters will do absolutely anything for a story that generates widespread interest, including telling lies about the information that they received and who they received it from. It has also been my experience that some reporters do have integrity and can be trusted. Unfortunately, being new in the area I have not yet learned who is who. Therefore, I have to assume the worst about all of them when it comes to this case. I will say this, I have read two articles so far and both have been very accurate, with the exception of spelling my name wrong. I know that when the media learns that the manner of death was salt poisoning they will become even more interested. I find it very curious that they have not looked into this case in more depth. I ask myself what ever happened to investigative reporting. The reporters in my area seem to be desk jockeys who investigate over the phone. One of the reporters called me and asked me what the cause of death was. I told her I could not discuss the case until after the trial. I suggested that she interview the baby's mother's family. She asked me what their name was. Again, I told her I could not discuss the case and she said ok and that was the end of that. Now, if you figure that the baby's mother has lived in a town of about 4,000 people her entire life it should not be hard to find out who her family is. How hard would it be for a reporter to walk around town and ask people? The funny thing about it is that her family knows all the details of the cause of death from the autopsy report. They also know a lot of the evidence in the case and other interesting details. I would think that about half a day of investigating would reveal one of the biggest stories this area has seen for quite some time. How often do you hear of a mother feeding a baby salt to poison it? It is very tempting to leak the information to a national paper or broadcast news agency. However, I know that if this story gets out it may cause problems with the prosecution. The defense does not have all of the knowledge of the case and any information that they get would only aid them in preparing their case. I am also very concerned about the limited experience that the small town prosecutors have, especially when dealing with a murder. The last murder case they handled was botched and they only got a second-degree conviction in a case where many people thought that the case was a slam-dunk for first-degree murder.

CHAPTER XVII
WHO LOVED THE BABY?

There are a lot of things about this case that raise questions in my mind. One of the most curious is if anyone really cared about this baby. I have two grandchildren and I know that if I learned that someone had murdered one of them I would be very interested in who did it and if the police were doing anything about it. In this case there have been no inquiries by anyone for more than six years. The mother has not shown any interest. The father has not called. None of the grandparents from either side have inquired about the case. There have been absolutely no objections that no one has been arrested. All of my inquiries about the family say that they are normally very vocal and do not sit still when something is wrong or someone is doing something to hurt a family member. As a matter of fact when the baby's mother was arrested the second time they were very vocal and critical. They objected strongly to what I was doing and me. Yet, where were they for the past six years while the case went unsolved? There are also law enforcement people in the family that have the connections to find out information about the case if they tried. When I ask myself why no one has raised any objections I can only come up with one reasonable answer, they know that the baby's mother killed the baby and there is no reason for them to ask who did it. This is especially true when it comes to the immediate family. Why did her mother just stand there when she was arrested for murder? She had a dejected look on her face and did not say one word. She did not object at all. I would think that if my daughter were being arrested for the murder of her baby, right in front of me, and I felt that she did not do it, I would be crazy with anger. That is, unless I knew she was guilty and there was nothing to object about. This was the impression that I got while I watched her mothers reaction. This is only my opinion of course; you can come to your own conclusions. While you are deciding remember that my jurisdiction is a very small town in a county that is run by the Sheriff's department. Remember that every time my department does something that the Sheriff's Department feels is wrong or inadequate they object and voice their opinions. Remember that the baby's mother has relatives who work there who you would think are very interested in this case but have shown absolutely no interest at all. Remember that there has been no criticism about this case by anyone other than one person in Social Services who deserves all the credit for this case being solved because she is the one who insisted that it be reopened. So, the answer to the question, "who loved the baby" is obvious, one lone social worker.

CHAPTER XVIII

THE TRIAL BEGINS

I appeared in Circuit Court today to testify in the first phase of the trial, a motion to suppress evidence hearing. The defense attorney was attempting to suppress the confession of the baby's mother so that it would not be allowed at trial. His main argument was that I tricked the baby's mother into confessing and that it should not be allowed. This is very important because the entire case depends on this confession of child abuse. Without it the case would weaken considerably. The only thing you are required to do in an interrogation is to provide the suspect with all of their rights. So long as you do not coerce them with physical force, all is fair. You can lie to them or deceive them in any way to get them to confess. The only thing that I did beyond questioning was to use the element of surprise when I arrested her and to exaggerate the evidence in some areas to convince her that she had no chance to get out of being convicted.

Fortunately the Judge saw through the defense attorney's attempt to discredit the confession and ruled that every thing that I did was proper and legal. The defense attorney asked for a lengthy continuance of the case of four to five months to give him time to prepare. The judge agreed that this was reasonable given all of the expert witnesses that he had to obtain and prepare for trial. I did not know at the time but the trial continued to be postponed for reasons you will read about in upcoming chapters. While I was writing this chapter some things happened to me that made my most fearful nightmares come true. Things that devastated me and my family, things caused by the States Attorney!

Chapter XIX

Suspicions

It seems that from the very first day of my involvement in this case things came up that made me suspicious of how this case was handled and how it seems to continue to be handled. When I first reviewed the file the first thing that I noticed is that there had never been an accusatory interview of anyone. The case seemed quite simple; there were only four possible suspects to look at yet no one ever accused any of them of anything. The only thing that came close was the polygraph test given to the baby's mother. This was probably the first suspicious thing that I saw and I did not even know it when I saw it. The original investigator told me that the polygraph operator came out of the room after the test and advised the baby's mother that she had passed the test. When I was told this I let it go for quite some time even though there was no written report in the file. After about a month I revisited the polygraph in order to obtain a copy of the report that should have been on file with the State Police. When I attempted to contact the trooper who conducted the test I could not get him to return my calls. I had to contact the quality control officer for the polygraph unit and request a copy of the report. When I spoke to him I advised him the person tested passed the test according to my information but I needed a copy of the report for my file. He called me back three days later and advised me that there was no report on file and that he would have to contact the operator and attempt to secure it. This went on for another week and no report was found. Finally, the control officer went to the archives and searched for the report. He did not find a report but he found a computer disc that contained the test information including the charts and questions. When he called me back and advised me of this I asked him if he had a chance to review the test and if he had an opinion as to truthful or deceptive. His response was that he wished I had not asked him that question. He stated that he had reviewed the test and also had three other people review it. They all came to the same conclusion. The baby's mother had been deceptive when she said that she did not shake the baby and deceptive about administering him salt. After a lot of pushing by me I finally received a written report of the polygraph. The report stated that the baby's mother was deceptive in these two areas. I have always been suspicious about why this report was never given to the police department and why the operator said that she had passed the test.

The assistant states attorney that was originally assigned this case refused to prosecute. He said that he had problems with several areas of the investigation. First, his information was that the baby's mother passed the polygraph test yet all the evidence seemed to point to her. Second, he stated that he had a conversation with the medical examiner that performed the autopsy and she made a statement to him that indicated that she would prepare her report any way that he wanted it. This really puzzles me, I have spoken to the same medical examiner and found her to be nothing but professional. The deposition that she gave was very informative and should have been very helpful to the prosecutor. According to the prosecutor the statement the medical examiner allegedly made lessened the credibility of the autopsy. I don't understand this either since two separate hospitals tests showed results that were very consistent with the autopsy results. The primary cause of death was salt poisoning and both hospitals lab tests confirmed potentially fatal levels of sodium. The prosecutor said that there was no evidence that definitively showed who gave salt to the baby and there were no incriminating statements by any of the suspects. Finally, the baby had so many medical problems that it would be a very difficult case to prove in court. When these opinions were related to the original investigator he was put in the position of not having the ability to do any further investigation. Even though there was ample probable cause to obtain an arrest warrant for child abuse, the states attorney did not want to deal with an arrest that would have to be dismissed by him in court. The feeling was that only a confession would adequately support any charges. Unfortunately it is very difficult to get a confession out of someone who is not under arrest. So, the case was left at this juncture. The states attorney had a position that the police had not collected enough evidence to prosecute and the police felt that the states attorney would not let them do their job and arrest the baby's mother. The baby's mother's statements gave more than enough probable cause for child abuse because she failed to obtain medical treatment in a timely fashion when the baby became very ill. This would have been cause for an arrest and an interview that probably would have resulted in her confession or at the very least more information to follow up on. It was getting obvious to me that the States Attorney was looking for reasons not to prosecute this case instead of looking for evidence he needed to obtain a conviction.

The next thing I noticed was that there were no medical records in the file except for the autopsy report. This is very unusual in this kind of investigation. I contacted Social Services to find out if I could get a copy of their medical records. I was told that the legal adviser for Social Services would not allow them to assist in this area because they were no longer working the case. The interesting thing is that the legal adviser is the same attorney who was the Assistant States Attorney that originally handled this case six years prior and refused to prosecute. Is this suspicious or just another coincidence? During my conversation with Social Services I was also advised that a doctor from Johns Hopkins Hospital was asked to review this case and that he did review it. His determination was that child abuse was evident. I asked for a copy of that report and was told that it was lost. I asked if that doctor had the medical records of the case and was told that he was given a copy to complete his review. When I said that I was going to contact him and obtain the records I was told that it would be of no use since his office reported that they lost them. Is this suspicious or just another coincidence?

When I was first assigned this case I was given a videotape of the deposition of the medical examiner. This tape was in the possession of the States Attorney's office at the time. When I found in the file a note that indicated that this deposition would take place I also noticed that depositions were scheduled for the doctors at the local hospital and for the social worker that interviewed the mother at Children's Hospital. I called Social Services and requested these deposition videos. Can you guess what I was told? They would have to confer with their legal adviser and get back to me. I was never given these tapes. They did not surface until the baby's mother was indicted and the States Attorney requested them from Social Services. Is this suspicious or just another coincidence?

It should be understood that my jurisdiction is a very small town in a very small county. The local politics run nearly everything that goes on. It seems that everyone is related to someone with authority of some kind. This case was no exception. The mother of the baby was the stepdaughter of a high ranking county official and the niece of a ranking member of the county sheriffs department. I found yet another note in the file regarding a disclosure by the assistant states attorney who worked this case. It seems that he discussed the autopsy report with the grandmother of the baby. This was done while the case was under investigation and the grandmother was considered a possible suspect by the police. I have also learned that a nurse that works for the health department also saw the autopsy report. This goes totally unexplained and makes little or no sense to anyone. Is this suspicious or coincidence?

It seems that there was another case involving the baby's mother and the baby's father. The baby's mother was working at a business and reported that it had been robbed. This turned out to be a false report that was concocted by the baby's father. It seems that he told her to report the robbery and they would take the money from the register. The father was arrested and charged but the mother was not. Again, the baby's mother is the stepdaughter, niece, oh well I think you get it by now. Is this suspicious or just another coincidence?

After the arrest had been made I was talking to the Assistant States Attorney who is now assigned to the case. She told me that her file on this case had disappeared. She said that it was gone for several days then reappeared. Is this suspicious or yet another coincidence?

There was also message left on my voice mail from the Assistant States Attorney. This was a call where she had fear in her voice and stated that she had to be careful with what she said in the company of others in her office. She was dealing with a lot of apprehension and a feeling that she was a target. It was hard for me to figure out if these feelings were caused by her involvement in this case or if there were underlying causes that had nothing to do with it. It really does not matter what was causing her anxiety, only that it was just another question of suspicion. I have returned to this page to add an interesting note. This assistant was promoted to Deputy just after this case concluded.

The interesting thing is that any one of these things can be explained away by some means. The problem is that when you are working a case such as this and you encounter all of these things you begin to think that there may be someone or something behind them. There is no way possible that I can point a finger of accusation at anyone regarding these issues.

I do think that it is important to be aware of them. If there is an effort by someone to stonewall the prosecution of this case it may be possible to connect all of the dots and determine who that person is. What you may find very interesting is that I am writing this book as it occurs.

I have returned to this chapter to add yet another suspicion to be considered. It is the day after the Grand Jury returned the indictment for murder and I am pondering the circumstances during the arrest. When the Sheriffs Department refused to allow me to be present during the arrest process I did not give it a lot of consideration in the beginning. Now, as I sit at my desk and think about it I realize that they prevented me from doing my job because I had arrested a family member of one of their deputies. There is no good reason why he could not have been removed from the situation until the processing was completed. This is just another case of suspicion or coincidence. When the States Attorney contacted the Sheriff and inquired about this he was told that they had just completed a large narcotics investigation and their arrest team had numerous arrests in the processing area. The relative of the baby's mother was a supervisor in charge of the operation and according to the Sheriff he had to be there. This sounds like a pretty good reason except that I know that it only would have taken a half an hour or less to process the baby's mother and her relative could have left for that much time if the Sheriff was that concerned. This is very indicative of small town politics in action. The unfortunate thing is that I have not been in this small town long enough to even care about the petty differences going on with the Sheriff's Department and my department. The fact of the matter is that the Sheriff's denial to allow me to be present may in fact be very important in the success or the failure of the prosecution of this case. It is not as if we have a murder every day and it should have taken precedence over their narcotics operation. At least for the very short time it would have taken.

I have absolutely no idea how it is all going to play out in the courts. I have a realistic point of view about this case. I feel that if I had never gone to work for the Police Department this case probably would never have been prosecuted. That would mean that the baby's mother would have never been arrested for what I believe was a brutal murder of an innocent baby. If she ultimately ends up serving any time in jail I will consider it to be a victory. It will be up to each individual to decide if justice is served. I only hope that my involvement in this case does not cause my family any kind of wrong doing in the future by members of the Sheriffs Department. I know that I will only be working here for a couple more years and then I have to live in their county every day. I have seen things happen to other people during my career because of someone in the law enforcement community attempting to exact revenge in any way that they can. I guess that I will have to deal with this if and when it happens. It is fortunate that most of the deputies are very professional as most law enforcement officers are and they probably would not stoop to such low tactics. Unfortunately for me I did not consider that the States Attorney could be as vindictive as he turned out to be.

There is another new development and I am sitting here this morning contemplating what has just happened in the City. We have just had a Mayoral election in the City and we have a new mayor. Problem is that the new mayor is a deputy on the County Sheriff's Department who lives in town. I wonder what affect, if any this may have on this case. The rift between my department and the sheriff's department is ever present and now one of their deputies is my mayor. He is also an investigator for their criminal investigative division and should have knowledge of this case. I wonder if he will have any criticism of how it was handled originally. There is also the connection of the baby's mother with his department. How will that influence anything that he may do or say? This is just another small thing in this case, but the small things just keep mounting and adding to the list of suspicions. My job is for the most part complete in this case. All that is left for me to do is to testify at the trial. All of the questions that I raise will hopefully be answered when the trial concludes. I am now in a waiting game since the trial will probably not be for another two months or more. As the legal process unfolds I am convinced that most of my questions will be answered one way or another.

It is yet another day and yet another question comes up. A particular assistant State's Attorney who had a very comprehensive understanding of all of its details originally reopened this case. The case was then taken over by the State's Attorney himself. His reason was that the assistant was pregnant and the birth of her baby would probably coincide with the trial. The State's Attorney then assigned it to another assistant because he was going out of town during the preliminary phases of the trial. The new attorney called me and wanted to know where the baby's mother's statement and the form that advised her of her rights were. He said that it was not in the file I gave them. I told him that I provided copies of everything in my file and that they were there when

I gave the file to the State's Attorney. It also seems that this attorney copied the entire file including confidential records from Social Services and investigative notes and was preparing to give it to the defense attorney. This would not only be a very bad thing to do from a prosecutorial sense but would also be a violation of the law. Social Services investigative reports are considered to be confidential and cannot be revealed. Fortunately the assistant who was originally assigned the case saw the secretary copying the file and inquired as to what it was for. I am thankful that someone competent was around that day.

It is very disruptive to my writing of this story to continue to find out about suspicious things. It seems as if every time I convince myself that coincidences are responsible something else surfaces to confuse the issue. As I have already said, most of the answers will not come until the case is concluded. In the meantime I will continue to write about the suspicions.

I am still seeing things occurring that I find to be unusual. I put in a letter to the States Attorney's office advising them that I would be on vacation during the month of July and that I would not be available for court. Thus far I have received two subpoenas for trial dates set in July for vary important cases. I called the States Attorney's office and advised them and was told not to worry about it and that they would advise the assigned attorney. When I checked with the assigned attorney three weeks later he said that he had not been told of the conflict. I suppose that this could happen on one occasion but it has now happened again and I am beginning to wonder why. A co-worker stated to me that it would not surprise him if they were trying to make me look bad by not showing up for scheduled trial dates. He has worked in the county for nearly 30 years and has seen many things during that time that would make him think that this is possible. He could not have been more right.

CHAPTER XX

JUSTICE?

I was involved in an arrest last week and the woman arrested went to the States Attorney's office and allegedly complained that I beat her up and choked her while she was handcuffed to the prisoner bench. This in itself would not normally disturb me because people make bogus complaints all the time when they get arrested. It seems that they think that if they complain about the arresting officer's actions it will lessen their charges some how. The interesting thing in this case is that without any corroborative evidence, or witnesses produced by this woman the States Attorney issued a subpoena two days later, demanding any video or audiotapes of the prisoner area during the time that she was arrested. Unfortunately for me there are no such tapes available. If there were I would have the necessary evidence to be exonerated of these false charges. I have never seen a States Attorney get involved in this kind of situation in this way, especially within two days of the incident occurring. Maybe I am becoming paranoid; I will let you be the judge of that. I can only say that I am very concerned these days and I have asked my Chief to keep me out of the limelight for a while. He has graciously agreed to this because he too has seen the inner workings of local politics and agrees that anything is possible.

Anything is possible; indeed, it has been more than two months since I last sat down to write. The reason for this is because I have been the subject of a Grand Jury investigation because of the complaint from the woman who said I beat and choked her. I was informed three days ago that I have been indicted for assault and malfeasance of office. I was arrested by the Sheriff's Department and processed by, guess who, the new Mayor of our town who is still a deputy. It looks like my previous suspicions are in fact realities. In my career as a police officer I have never seen anything like this before. I have consulted with two different attorneys' who agree that the State has a very weak case, if any case at all. The complaining woman has a long record and a past history of making false reports of persons assaulting her. She has no witnesses or evidence to support her allegations yet the States Attorney has pursued charges against me. I have been told that she is an informant for the County Narcotics Task Force and has been used several times to obtain probable cause for their search warrants and related drug investigations.

My greatest fear has come true, I have been charged with a crime. I have given this much thought and I cannot figure out what the motivating factor is that has driven the States Attorney to seek this indictment against me. It is very clear that it is not because he thinks that I have committed the crime. There is no evidence against me except for the word of someone who has absolutely no credibility as a witness. I am thinking if you wonder why the States Attorney was so reluctant in charging the baby's mother when there was overwhelming evidence against her yet he is so willing and aggressive to charge me when it is clear that he has no evidence to convict me of the crime. This brings up another question, what evidence has been manufactured to support his case against me. I have to feel that this is the case. It is almost impossible to believe that the States Attorney would charge a police officer with a crime unless he had sufficient evidence to convict him. The only other reasonable theory is that he plans to drop the charges at the last minute and only wishes to put me through the agony and great expense of mounting a criminal defense. I wonder if he is doing this only because he is angry at the embarrassment I caused him during my investigation of this case or is there still another motive that is connected to his lack of desire to convict the murderer of a three-month-old baby. What is the skeleton in his closet that would give him reason for this? Regardless of the answer I am put in the position of defending myself against bogus charges and my concern for convicting the baby's mother has diminished greatly for the time being. I have been totally devastated by these charges. After my family, police work has been the love of my life and it feels like I have lost a close family member with what turns out to be the death of my career. No matter how this turns out my career is over. My wife has insisted that I no longer be a police officer and that she will no longer support me if I do. I can't say that I blame her one bit. She has been through a lot over the years and has always stood by me no matter what. I am having great difficulty dealing with the fact that I have always policed within the Constitution and the Bill of Rights. I have always given everyone the benefit of the doubt. I have never been found to use any unnecessary or excessive force during my career and I have not so much as one small black mark on my record. To have my career end like this is something that I will never come to terms with. I guess the States Attorney wins no matter what happens from here out. It is a shame that so much power is given to one man to abuse and use for his own means and satisfaction.

As I continue to struggle through this case I still have many unanswered questions about why things are happening the way that they are. I don't know if these questions will be answered or not and I can only wait to see how the trial plays out. I now wonder if there will even be a trial. Will the States Attorney say that I have been discredited as a witness and drop the charges against the baby's mother? What an upsetting thought that is. It is however a realistic possibility given what has happened in the past two months.

There are other very interesting things happening as well. I found out that an armed robbery case of mine was adjudicated without me. Apparently the States Attorney agreed to a plea agreement where the defendant was allowed to plead guilty and receive only the time he has already served in jail as his sentence. So, in effect he got about seven months in jail for committing an armed robbery. Quite a deal, don't you think? I have another armed robbery case scheduled for next week where the suspect is a career criminal with several prior convictions for robbery. I can only wonder what will happen in this case. There is still another armed robbery of a hotel where the suspect is incarcerated in another county jail. He has fully confessed to me to robbing two hotels in my town. I have charged him with the crimes but I have not heard anything about the trial. It is apparent that The States Attorney does not wish to prosecute this career criminal who has spent most of his life in prison. His reason is probably that he already is facing charges in the other jurisdiction that will put him in jail for the rest of his life and he does not want to spend the taxpayers' money prosecuting him. He is however not reluctant to spend that money on prosecuting me for a crime where no evidence exists. It will be very interesting to see how all of these cases play out. One thing is for sure though; justice in this small town is very strange indeed.

After the Grand Jury returned an indictment in my case my Chief had a conversation with the States Attorney and he commented that it was only an indictment, not a conviction. What do you suppose he meant by that? I took it as meaning that he never intended to convict me but only to put me through the process of being charged. He also told the Chief that my case would be set for trial after the baby's mother's trial so that my charge would not be a problem. That plan has not worked out for him either. The baby's mother's attorney filed for a continuance stating that he has not had enough time and the case is now destined to be tried after my case. I now wonder if my case will also be continued by the States Attorney causing it to be drug out even further.

I used to think that I knew the meaning of justice. Now I wonder if I will ever understand what justice really is. I have also learned that trying to figure out God's plan is an exercise in futility. There has been several times during my investigation of this case that I thought His plan was for me to solve the murder and find justice for the baby. I can now see that the plan is far greater than that and I give great thought about how it will all play out in the end or even if it will ever be revealed to me.

My story has now taken a side road to deal with my own prosecution by the States Attorney and all that is involved with it. I am now awaiting the trial of the woman who accused me. She has to face charges from where she was arrested on that day. She has also been charged with an unrelated assault during the past week and is facing eviction from her residence. Her already tarnished credibility is becoming even more tainted by her actions of late. When she was scheduled to appear in court to answer the charges placed against her in my case she was asked by the judge if she had an attorney. She stood up and stated that she was a witness in another case and that the States Attorney was her attorney. One of the States Attorney's assistants was handling the case but the States Attorney was in the courtroom. As a matter of fact when he came in he sat down right beside me even though the courtroom was practically empty. When she made this statement to the judge the States Attorney got up and hurried to the prosecutor and whispered something in his ear. The States Attorney then took over and told the judge that he would not oppose a continuance so that she could get an attorney. I have never heard of the States Attorney personally involved in a case where the defendant was charged with disorderly conduct and resisting arrest. An assistant would almost always handle this.

I also appeared in court when she was supposed to be tried for another assault case that was completely unrelated to me, the police department or anyone else for that matter. It was a case where a woman filed a complaint against her and a summons was issued for assault. When her case was called she did not answer and the States Attorney went to bat for her again. He recommended to the judge that subpoenas be reissued because she had recently moved. The judge did not buy this and issued a warrant for her arrest. You can probably already guess that this warrant never was issued. The States Attorney arranged for her to be located and convinced the judge to recall the warrant. It is very interesting how the States Attorney keeps protecting her.

On the day of her trail to face the charges that were placed against her the day she accused me of assaulting her I went to court to observe. It was interesting that the States Attorney was on the docket to handle all cases in the courtroom that day and handled the first three that were called. Then this woman's case was called and one of his assistants took over and handled her case. Apparently a plea bargain was agreed to and she pled guilty to disorderly conduct and the resisting arrest charge was dropped by the State. This is a normal plea bargain in this kind of case. What was unusual is that when the Judge sentenced her, after being informed of a prior conviction for the same charge, he stated "I sentence you to fifteen days in the County jail and a term of probation for"- the assistant States Attorney then jumped up and stated to the judge that the State was not seeking any active term of incarceration. The Judge paused then continued saying that he was suspending the fifteen days in jail and she would be placed on eighteen months of probation. There is no good reason for the Assistant States Attorney to do what he did except that the States Attorney was protecting her from jail time in reward for helping him to prosecute me. This action is in direct conflict with what the States Attorney told the judge during a previous appearance. He told the judge that the woman was receiving no special consideration regarding her charges just because she was a State's witness in my case. The involved officers approached me after the trial and neither of them could believe what had happened. With a prior conviction in this County she would have normally gone to jail for some amount of time, and it took the protection of the States Attorney to keep her out of jail. It is still so very unbelievable to me that the States Attorney would coddle and protect this woman who has a long history in the legal system and who has been previously convicted of crimes, and at the same time prosecute a career police officer with an exemplary record when he had no viable evidence to do so. It certainly makes a logically minded person suspect that there is indeed something behind his actions other than doing his job. Since my only dealings with him during my time here was the murder case and the dealings were very negative to say the least, I have to conclude that it the two are certainly connected.

Where is the justice here? I am told that no matter how my trial turns out I have no recourse against the States Attorney because he has prosecutorial immunity. It is very hard for me to accept this. I don't see how someone in an elected position can abuse his authority with absolutely no recourse. He has put me through a living hell for more than seven months. He has caused my entire family to go through very unnecessary anxiety while they worry about what is going to happen to me. Even though I know that the evidence will support my innocence, it is hard to not think about the possibility that the corruption extends to the judges. I only pray that this is not the case. I can't stop thinking about when I called my wife and told her that I had been indicted. The anguish in her voice was the most heartbreaking thing I have ever heard from her. The tears that followed for more than seven months gave me the most helpless feeling I have ever had. The ordeal of having to face my children with this news was one of the most difficult things I have ever done. When I saw the heartbreak in their eyes it devastated me. I have always lived my life trying to help people at every opportunity. I have put my life on the line numerous times for strangers. I have done one of the most difficult jobs without ever being questioned about my integrity, honesty or loyalty to the citizens whom I served every day. I have never asked for anything in return more than a paycheck and benefits for my family and I have no regrets. All this being said I still wonder how one man can have the power to do this to me without any accountability to anyone. If this is justice we have a serious problem. Unfortunately I have not found any solutions other than to campaign for the States Attorney's opponent in the next election.

CHAPTER XXI

MY TRIAL

When you are unjustly charged with a crime it is a devastating situation. It greatly affects your family who worry about you and what may happen. During this ordeal my wife was tortured every day with the thought that I may end up in jail. She has heard the stories about how judges are particularly hard on police officers when they are convicted of any crime. My daughters are also concerned about this along with the daily concerns of helping their mother deal with the situation. All the people you know change when they see you on the news and hear that you were arrested and charged with a crime. If it were not for the total support of my pastor during this time I don't know what we would have done. You really find out what people in your life are truly important when you go through something like this. Your true friends, like family, stand by you with total support and belief in your innocence. You also are able to identify some people who come forward in their support of you, people who you did not know before and are also your true friends.

When the States Attorney first got involved in the investigation of the allegations against me it was June 6th. His actions were as obvious to me as I am sure they will be to you. The first thing he did was drag out a Grand Jury for two months in my case. I have never heard of such a thing. He then scheduled my trial for November 7th, a very long time to wait in a jurisdiction that is not exactly a busy one. The case was then continued by the State until January 9th and I was left hung out to dry for more than seven months. He also added supposed other crimes that were presented to the Grand Jury but there was no indictment against anyone but me. When I received the Grand Jury testimony against me it was very clear that he worked very hard to get an indictment against me. The questions he asked were very leading in nature and resulted in expected answers. I will even say that if I were on the Grand Jury I would have indicted myself.

When the States Attorney first had me indicted he stated that he was going to handle the prosecution personally. This pleased my attorney because the States Attorney is not known for being a good trial attorney. A few weeks prior to my trial date my attorney was notified of two additional State's witnesses. One of them was the States Attorney's daughter. I can tell you with total certainty that she had no knowledge of my case. The only logical reason for her being listed would be to create a conflict for the States Attorney so that he would not have to prosecute this loser of a case. About a week later my attorney got a call from the States Attorney informing him that he was giving the case to one of his assistants, surprise! The assistant was also a just hired new Assistant States Attorney with very little trial experience.

I find it very interesting that the States Attorney would go after a career police officer with an unblemished record in a situation that looks suspicious in the first place and assign it to his very newest assistant, unless, of course, he expected to lose the case in the first place.

I really expected that the States Attorney's plan was to torment me for seven months just to teach me a lesson and then drop the charges at the last minute. He could have very easily done this and saved face in the process. He would only have to blame the lack of credibility of his only witness against me and say that he had only recently found out how bad she really was. Three days prior to my trial a written plea offer was received from the States Attorney. He offered to recommend probation before judgment if I pled guilty. This would mean that I would ultimately not have a criminal record. A condition of the plea bargain was that I resign from the police department. This sends a very strong message to me and verifies all of my suspicions and accusations against the States Attorney in my own mind. His plan was to get rid of me from the beginning. The only question that remains is it because of the murder investigation and his unwillingness to prosecute the baby's mother or is it because I bruised his fragile little ego, you choose because I still don't know.

I had an occasion to call the Assistant States Attorney who is again handling the murder case. The case has been dragged out so long that she has had her baby and returned to work. Not only did the case get reassigned to her but she received a promotion to Deputy Assistant as well. This puzzles me greatly since my last conversation with her prior to her maternity leave was one where she was afraid that she was going to lose her job. The chief witness in her murder case has now been charged with a crime by her boss and he has given the case back to her to prosecute. Anyway, during our conversation I asked her if she knew the woman who had complained about me and she stated, "Yes I do, that lying no good bitch." I asked her what she was talking about and she told me that she had handled an assault case about four years earlier. In that case the woman had accused her boyfriend of brutally assaulting her. She reported to an officer on my department both on the phone and in person. She followed up the report with letters to the Assistant States Attorney that stated she wanted to fully prosecute her boyfriend this time. When the case came to trial she told the Assistant States Attorney that she changed her mind and no longer wanted to prosecute him. This made her angry and she called her as a witness anyway in hope that she would commit perjury and could be prosecuted. This is exactly what happened. The only problem is that the judge was angered by this and admonished her in open court for putting a witness on the stand that everyone knew was going to lie. She also told me that when she returned to her office the States Attorney also yelled at her and said that the judge had called him to complain.

What is most interesting about this is that it verifies that the States Attorney had prior knowledge about how this woman lies and has absolutely no credibility yet he used her and only her to have me indicted for criminal charges. This leaves no doubt in my mind that he had other motives to indict me. The question that is still unanswered is weather or not his motive was to discredit me, as a witness in the murder case so that he would have an excuse not to prosecute, or weather his ego is so large that he was just getting even with me for criticizing him and forcing him to do his job. I have been able to find many supporters of both theories.

The day after I had the conversation with the Assistant States Attorney I got a call from my Chief. He said that the States Attorney had called him and asked him to tell me not to discuss my case with his assistants. Even though the Assistant States Attorney, who I thought was my friend, guaranteed me that she would not repeat our conversation, this proves that she too cannot be trusted. Little did she and her boss know that my attorney had already requested a subpoena for her to testify about the story she told me? My attorney also told me that if she had done her job and charged the woman with perjury I would never have been charged because under State law she would no longer be allowed to testify under oath if convicted of perjury. I guess this is just another example of this States Attorney's office failing to do their jobs.

When my trial date arrived no sign of the charges being dropped surfaced and the trial commenced. The Assistant States Attorney put her case on and everyone in the courtroom was wondering why we were there. The woman who accused me lied on the stand about several things brought out by my attorney. Her testimony was so unbelievable that the judge winced on several occasions. Her basic story was that I entered the room where she was handcuffed to a bench and for no reason approached and slapped her across the face harder than she had ever been hit in her life. She then said that I used a secret police chokehold with my thumbs and choked her into unconsciousness. She had produced photos of bruises on her face that she said were caused by me striking her. The problem was that in two of the photos she was dressed completely differently, including jewelry, than in the other photos. This was something that was suggested by my daughter when my attorney was preparing for my defense. She said that we should check photos and compare them to the mug shot taken the night of the arrest. My daughter, being the fashion guru that she is stated that if the photos were taken at different times her clothing or jewelry might be different. Sure enough, in two of the photos that were presented during the trial that she testified were both taken just after her arrest she was wearing earrings in one and not the other. This was a key issue in discrediting her testimony against me. She testified that all of the photos were taken the night she was released from custody and that she did not go anywhere else prior to the photos. When the State rested my attorney requested a judgment of acquittal due to the lack of evidence. The judge denied this request with obvious reluctance in his voice. I was then called to testify and told what happened. I testified that the woman was being very loud and disruptive to the entire police station. She was yelling at the top of her voice and could be heard even upstairs in the public lobby where people were trying to conduct business. I approached her and attempted to get her to quiet down and she ignored me. She would not even make eye contact with me and she continued yelling threats against the officers that arrested her. In an attempt to gain her attention I took my hand and slapped the concrete wall over her head. This startled her and she stopped yelling. I think that in fact she thought I was going to strike her. As soon as she realized what I had done she went back to yelling.

Knowing that she was not going to stop I walked away and instructed the officers to deal with her as fast as possible and get her out of the station.

When she was taken before the District Court Commissioner for a bond hearing the woman accused me of beating her up. She pointed to her face and asked the Commissioner if he saw the marks on her. The Commissioner told her he did not see any marks and testified to that at my trial. This was an important part of my defense. If I would have struck her as she described it would have left redness and certainly bruises that would have been visible an hour later. This combined with the photos that she produced that were obviously taken at a different time, and her previous record of lying, made the decision easy for the judge. As a matter of fact when the defense side of the trial was being held we decided to end it about one third of the way through our witnesses because it was so obvious that she was lying and had made up the entire story. The judge agreed and his decision was instantaneous. He stated that it was a "no brainer" and criticized the lack of credible evidence against me just prior to finding me not guilty.

There is another interesting thing that occurred during my testimony at my trial. The Assistant States Attorney asked me about my home address. When I first moved to the area I got a post office box at the post office and the address was different than my home address. I still don't know why she asked about this. I can only conclude that maybe she thought I would deny it and she could catch me in a lie. I told her that I only had the box for about a year and a half and had not had it for more than six years. Then she asked me if I thought that I was charged in this case by the States Attorney because of something that had happened during my investigation of a murder case. This took me by surprise and I could not imagine why she was asking this question. My answer was almost immediate though and I stated that I absolutely thought so. She then asked me if I had talked about this with someone recently, meaning the Assistant States Attorney. Although my answer to this question was also immediate, the thought ran through my mind that when I talked to the Assistant States Attorney about ten days earlier she told me that our conversation would be confidential. It was clearly evident to me that she had gone back to the States Attorney and told him about the conversation and since the States Attorney was just informed that she was now on my witness list he became furious with her. I answered the question yes and she let go of it at that point. I think that she was again trying to get me to lie by saying that I did not have the conversation. It is amazing how these country bumpkins think us city folk are so stupid. Can you imagine that?

My Chief has tried very, very hard to convince me to come back to work for him. I resigned the day after my trial. It is my position that the States Attorney, given the chance, would come after me again. The best thing I can do is work to get him defeated in the upcoming election and live off my pension check. This is what I will do. I am also very concerned with the lack of support I received from my department, including my Chief. He told me that he wanted to do a press release in support of me but that he was instructed not to do so by the town manager. I realize that he is in the twilight of his career and ready to retire but if I were in his place I could not be held back from supporting one of my men that I knew was being unjustly prosecuted. The department is also not associated with any fraternal order of police. If they were it would be a totally different situation. I know that they would bring this case to the attention of the press in a way that would be very supportive of me. I have seen this before and it has a very positive affect on how the States Attorney proceeds. The FOP is a very powerful organization when it comes to election issues and the States Attorney knows this well. I attempted to solicit the support of the State FOP Lodge but I was told that they would not get involved since I was no longer an active member. This was very disappointing to me considering the fact that I was a member in good standing during my entire first career and I never needed their support then.

I did, however, go and see a civil attorney to find out if I could file suit against the States Attorney for his malicious prosecution of me. I had some doubts when I did this because I am still within the rural community where everyone knows everyone and I wondered from the start it the attorney would have integrity or not. I paid him for a consultation and explained my story. When I was through his response was that the story was truly unbelievable and that I had indeed suffered a great injustice. He said that he needed to research the law that was applicable to the case but it looked on the surface to be a case that he was interested in taking on. He told me that he would contact me in a couple of weeks to let me know. After a month went by without hearing from him I called and left a message but got no response. I called again with the same result and then sent an e-mail that was also ignored. After two months went by I called and complained to the receptionist and she connected me with the attorney's assistant who assured me that he would call me back. I waited three days without hearing from him so I called her again. She said that the attorney had written me a letter and that the letter would explain everything. It seems that the attorney's position is that the States Attorney has prosecutorial immunity and cannot be sued. I may be wrong but I would think that he would have known this well enough to tell me when we met and he took my money. The fact that he ignored me for more than two months and refused to respond to my calls leads me to conclude that there is some underlying cause for his actions. Gee, does that sound familiar or what! Well here I go again looking for justice in all the wrong places. My long time negative opinion of lawyers has just been reinforced.

CHAPTER XXII
THE MURDER TRIAL

It has been two weeks since the conclusion of my trial. I received a subpoena for the murder trial and it is scheduled for next month. I have been waiting to hear from the States Attorney's office to schedule the meeting with them for the purpose of trial preparation. This is a very important meeting that should have already occurred. The trial is only three weeks away and if anything comes up that needs to be addressed it leaves very little time. The first thing I think of is all of the incompetence I have witnessed over the past two years and that is probably why I have not heard from them. I talked to the victim witness coordinator in their office the other day and she told me that the States Attorney is very angry with the Assistant who is handling this case. He is upset because she talked to me and caused herself to be subpoenaed for my case. She is probably hesitant to call me for this reason and I am very apprehensive about dealing with anyone in the States

Attorney's office at this point. I will do what I have to do though and hope that I don't become a target again.

I have been very tempted to go to the press about this case and give them the story. The story of how a 3 month old baby was murdered by its mother and how the States Attorney did not arrest her or even insist on an aggressive investigation. Tell them about how the States Attorney let the case sit inactive for six years until I began to investigate it. Let it be known that the States Attorney resisted all of my efforts to arrest the mother and how I had to practically badger him into letting me obtain a warrant. Tell them how the States Attorney got angry with me and used the complaint of someone he knew to be a liar from past cases to have me indicted and charged with a crime. How he pursued the case with no evidence against me all the way through the criminal trial where the judge criticized his prosecution of the case. Tell them how he also tried to prosecute another officer who was listed as one of my witnesses, and how the judge also criticized him in this case as he found the officer not guilty. I wonder what they would do with the story. The only problem is that I know that it is not in the best interest of the case to let the press in prior to the trial. Even though I suspect that the States Attorney is not intending to fully prosecute the case I have to do my job in its entirety.

I am sitting in my home office writing and thinking about the fact that I still have not heard from the States Attorneys office about a pre-trial meeting. This is a first-degree murder trial with a file that is more than a foot thick and a dozen or more witnesses and it is only three weeks prior to the trial.

On the date that the trial was scheduled I appeared in court and I was approached by the Assistant States Attorney who told me that I was not needed because they were only going to have a scheduling hearing to set a firm date for the trial. This was because the defense had filed a motion with the court stating that they needed a lot of evidence that had not yet been provided to them and they wanted the case continued. It seems that the defense attorney wants to bring several expert witnesses in to testify to matters concerning shaken baby syndrome and others to testify about the ability of salt being used as a poison. This of course means that the States Attorney must bring in its own witnesses to counter the defense's claims. What this really means to me is that the trial will be lengthy and very complicated. This is a common ploy used by defense lawyers to try to confuse the jury as much as possible with technical testimony. We all saw this ploy in the O.J. case where it worked very well and caused O.J. to be acquitted.

Scheduling hearings are normally held in the judge's chambers and not in open court, on the record. The Judge in this case is the same judge that sat on my trial and he ordered that the scheduling hearing be held in court, on the record. When the hearing was over he even told the court stenographer to type out the transcript and put it in the file. These are all very unusual acts and I can only suspect that the judge is beginning to suspect that something is suspicious about the way this case has progressed. He further stated that he was going to have the case set before a visiting judge because of the case's history. This statement was referring to my trial and the suspicious nature of it and the statements that I made during my testimony that I believed that I was only charged as a result of conflict with the States Attorney in this case. The judge then ordered that a motions hearing be set two months from now so that a ruling on the defense's motion could take place. He then set a firm trial date of October 10th, more than seven months away. This case is already eight years old and I keep running into delay after delay. It sounds like this time the case will be resolved in one way or another when the next trial date arrives. The thing that keeps going through my mind is what will happen between now and the trial date. I wonder if the States Attorney will try any other tactics against me or if he will be satisfied to let the case run its course. I can only wait and see.

Well, I did not have to wait for very long. When I went to the motions hearing the Assistant States Attorney was talking to me about the case and he said the States Attorney said to say hello to me and to tell me that if he lost the election this year he was going to move to the county I lived in and run for office there. Now if anyone has even the slightest doubt that the charges against me were motivated by personal reasons of the States Attorney, you should no longer feel that way. What a very unprofessional display of conduct to continue to rub salt into an already festered wound.

The motion hearing was very interesting. The States public defender had secured the assistance of the forensic expert in their office. She filed a motion of discovery to receive evidence that she thought was being held back by the States Attorney. This was not the case. I supplied the States Attorney with everything in the case except for personal investigator's notes that are not required by law to be turned over. The judge basically ruled and ordered the States Attorney to review the file again and turn over anything to the defense that they were entitled to. The defense also had a motion to obtain records from Social Services relevant to their investigations of the baby's father for child abuse against his other son. The judge denied this motion because the files are protected under the law.

The States Attorney told me that he offered a plea to the public defender. He offered to accept a plea of guilty to manslaughter and child abuse. This would have been a very good deal since the total penalty for both of these is thirty years (fifteen years each), and the mother has already confessed to two counts of child abuse that carries the exact same penalties. Considering the fact that she has no prior criminal convictions she probably would have had to do five years or less of actual jail time. They turned the deal down. They know of course that they will probably be offered the same deal on the day of trial.

The trial is now set for five months from now and I am told that the date is in stone. I know however that a lot of things could cause further delays. I almost hope that something does and the trial is held after the election in November and we have a new States Attorney in office.

Two months have passed and I have received a notice to appear for another motions hearing. The defense is continuing to hack away at the system in an obvious attempt to build a case for appeal. The more that they ask for, weather they are entitled to it or not, the more chance that they may happen on a circumstance that would justify an appeal if they lose.

The motions' hearing was very routine for the most part. The defense asked for things that they were not entitled to, such as Social Services reports, and the judge denied them. The very last point that they made was a request for a copy of the letter sent to the States Attorney by the mother's cellmate while she was in jail. They found that it existed in some notes that they were given during discovery. The assistant States Attorney said that he did not know about the letter. This was very interesting to me. I actually read the letter prior to the Grand Jury. The States Attorney had it in his possession. This is yet another example of the incompetence of the States Attorney's office. An important piece of evidence like this should be handled very carefully and I can't believe that the Assistant who is handling the case has no knowledge of it. I even referred to it in my report of investigation. Curiously the request for the discovery of the letter was not included in the defense's motion for that day and the judge denied anything related to it until another motion is filed. This means yet another court date prior to the actual trial. When we returned to court to address this and other issues I was called into the prosecutor's office and he told me that he was going to drop the murder charges against the baby's mother. He said, "The doctors are turning against us". When I asked him to explain he said that the doctor who examined the baby's eyes was changing his opinion about the cause of the retinal hemorrhages. He now has the opinion that the injuries may have been caused by another existing condition that the baby had. The prosecutor also said that the defense attorney had interviewed this doctor and turned him into a defense witness. He went on to say that when he contacted the medical examiner that performed the autopsy she also began to waiver in her opinion. I found all of this to be very suspicious since both of these doctors had given sworn depositions and stated very conclusively that the baby suffered from shaken baby syndrome. When I tried to suggest other alternatives it was obvious from the prosecutor's responses that he had no interest in proceeding with the murder charge. This is something that has existed since the death of the baby; the State's Attorney's office has never had any desire to prosecute the baby's mother. I only wish that I knew the real reason why!

It was very curious when we went into the courtroom and the prosecutor dropped the murder charge. There was absolutely no reaction from the baby's mother or any of her family. It was clearly as if they knew it was coming. What was really surprising is that her attorney did react with surprise. This is yet another thing that makes be believe that the baby's mother is somehow directly connected to the State's Attorney's office.

When the day of the actual trial came I felt very uneasy and unprepared. I still had not had a conference with the prosecutor to discuss my testimony. This is something that is unheard of in a case such as this one. When I arrived he called me into his office and told me that he was proceeding with the child abuse charges. I asked him who was going to testify for us and he said that two of the doctors involved were there. I found out later that the two doctors were the doctors who were subpoenaed by the defense as their witnesses. The prosecutor had no one else to testify for the State. He had no one to give expert testimony about shaken baby syndrome, even though this was the basis for the child abuse charge against the baby's mother. He had no one from the medical examiners office to testify as to the injuries revealed in the autopsy. He did not have the cellmate of the baby's mother there to testify about being told that the baby was given salt in its formula. I knew before the trial started that we had absolutely no chance to get a conviction. The second charge of child abuse was a result of the baby's mother failing to get medical treatment for the baby when he became very ill after being shaken. The prosecutor had no intention of even pursuing this charge because he said the time was not long enough. This was also interesting because of the baby's history of illness. This was a baby who had heart and liver problems and had been very ill since birth. The mother's statement to me was that the baby was very ill and not responsive. She also said that the baby had thrown up several times. With a baby that is this ill it is unthinkable that she would deny medical treatment for nearly three hours. The only logical reason for that would be that she wanted the baby to die.

The entire trial took less than two hours. I was only on the witness stand for fifteen minutes for a case that I worked on for nearly a year. When the State rested its case the defense made a motion for acquittal and the judge granted it saying that the State had not proven shaken baby syndrome. This was the worst prosecutorial effort that I have ever seen. I have seen drunk driving cases get far more attention. I must say that again the baby's mother and her family did not seem surprised by this outcome. There was no cheering, hugging, or any outward sign of emotion. There is no question that they knew what was going on from the beginning. This entire prosecution was put on for my benefit and a not guilty means that the baby's mother was free and clear and could not be charged again.

The totality of this case overwhelms me with suspicion. I am left to wonder why the States Attorney was so obvious in his lack of effort to prosecute the baby's mother. Many questions are left unanswered. Did he owe a debt to someone in her family or was he just doing them a favor? Does someone in her family have something on him and pressured him into his lack of prosecutorial effort? Is it possible that it was all a part of his well-known vindictive nature and his desire to hurt me in any way possible, just because I bruised his ego when I criticized his office? There are many people that believe this is the case, though I believe that it goes farther than just a vindictive act. I truly believe in my heart that the States Attorney was motivated by some personal or political gain. The unfortunate thing is that I have no proof of this and I can't say that it is so with any certainty.

Any way that you look at it someone has gotten away with the murder of a very small defenseless infant. The only satisfaction at all is to know that person has to live with what they have done and will have to answer for it in a higher place.

I find that I get very little peace from this thought.

Final Thoughts

I know that the States Attorney will be upset if he reads this book. The voters who elected him should ask him why he let this case go without prosecution in the first place. He will say there was a lack of evidence. I will tell you that he had the baby's mother indicted for murder based only on the evidence that was present when I took the case. The death of an infant that was declared a homicide by the medical examiner should not be taken lightly. He is the chief law enforcement officer in the county and there was not even a police report of investigation in the case. This would have at least organized all the material such as statements, medical reports, etc. I can't even begin to fathom how this can happen.

He should also be asked why he prosecuted me without evidence more than the word of a person that he knew through experience was not truthful in past cases prosecuted by his office. He will tell you that he believed her and that he was only doing his job based on a grand jury indictment. I will tell you that he was the one who presented the case to the grand jury and that he slanted his presentation in a way that he would get the indictment against me.

Thirdly, he should be asked why he failed to prosecute the baby's mother for at least child abuse. The case his office presented during this trial did not even have a witness to testify what shaken baby syndrome is, the secondary cause of death of the baby and the mother confessed to shaking the baby within the time frame set by the medical examiner. I have seen drunk-driving cases prosecuted with more vigor than that trial was. I am sure that he will tell you that he presented the evidence that he had. I will tell you that he did not try to convict her. A statement made by the prosecuting assistant states attorney to my Lieutenant backs this up, "my heart just wasn't in this case". You decide why that would be.

It has been nearly two years since I finished this story and I have not picked it up until now. I am now completely retired and my wife and I are enjoying life with my children and grandchildren. I still think about this case nearly every day and I find it ironic that not only the baby's mother has to live with what she has done, but I also live with doubts about the way I handled the case. I often wonder if I could have or should have done some things differently. I still read the local paper on line in hopes of finding some story about justice in this case. The States Attorney is still in office and I wonder if justice will come his way. The baby's mother no longer has custody of any children, which is probably a good thing, and I do get some measure of satisfaction from this. I have finally let go of all the anger that I harbored for more than four years. This is why I have decided to finally finish my story and attempt to publish it. This is only one story of a brutal act that seems to go unpunished. I think that it is important for people to know that this kind of thing happens every day and maybe this knowledge will help someone else to recognize another injustice and do something to resolve it. I pray that they also recognize the fact that there is seldom true justice on earth and that we will all be truly judged in the end.

LaVergne, TN USA
06 December 2009
166114LV00003BC/241/P